Praise for *Striking Back*

"Aaron Klein's book is a gripping, real-life spy drama, a fascinating account of one of the opening battles in the current jihad."
—ZEV CHAFETS, author of *Heroes and Hustlers, Hard Hats and Holy Men: Inside the New Israel*

"Fast-paced . . . Klein's book, through new revelations, gives his readers a much sharper look at the incident in Munich and the hunt for those guilty in the years that followed."
—Framingham *MetroWest Daily News*

"Sober, accurate and balanced . . .The telling details and Klein's straightforward writing imbues *Striking Back* with all the suspense and intrigue of the best spy novel, shining light on the shadowy worlds of terrorism, covert operations and assassination."
—*Contra Costa Times*

"Skillfully shows how the media can play an independent hand in history . . . The way Klein describes the role of publicity is relevant in America as we debate intelligence gathering and privacy in our own war on terror." —*Creative Loafing Charlotte*

STRIKING BACK

STRIKING BACK

THE 1972 MUNICH OLYMPICS MASSACRE
AND ISRAEL'S DEADLY RESPONSE

AARON J. KLEIN

Translated from the Hebrew
by Mitch Ginsburg

RANDOM HOUSE TRADE PAPERBACKS

NEW YORK

ISBN 978-0-8129-7463-8

LIBRARY OF CONGRESS CATALOGING-IN-PUBLICATION DATA
Klein, Aaron J.
    Striking back: the 1972 Munich Olympics Massacre and
Israel's deadly response / Aaron J. Klein.—1st ed.
        p.   cm.
    Includes index.
    ISBN 978-0-8129-7463-8
        1. Munaòòamat Aylål al-Aswad.   2. Terrorism—Germany—
    Munich.   3. Olympic Games (20th: 1972: Munich, Germany)
    4. Athletes—Violence against—Germany—Munich.
    5. Israelis—Violence against—Germany—Munich.   6. Revenge.
    7. Terrorism—Prevention.   8. Israel. Mosad le-modi°'n
    òe-tafòidim meyuòadim.   I. Title.

HV6433.G32M855   2005
364.152'30943364—dc22   2005057401

Printed in the United States of America

www.atrandom.com

9 8

Photo researcher/editor: Ziv Koren

In memory of my late father,

Alexander S. Y. Klein,

who taught me the value of humility

and the meaning of integrity

From the blood-drenched history of the Jewish

nation, we learn that violence which begins

with the murder of Jews, ends with the spread of

violence and danger to all people, in all nations.

We have no choice but to strike at terrorist

organizations wherever we can reach them.

That is our obligation to ourselves and to peace.

—ISRAELI PRIME MINISTER GOLDA MEIR, 1972

CONTENTS

STRIKING BACK

1 TWENTY YEARS LATER

The white Jeep Renegade hurtled down A-22 on its way to Paris. The driver was alone in the vehicle. He stopped twice, to buy food from a vending machine and gas from a pump. Five hours later, his surveillance tail almost lost him in the swirling rush-hour traffic of a Paris afternoon. On Rue du Commandant Mouchotte the trackers watched the new Renegade with the German plates, B-585X, make a sudden right turn. The driver of the surveillance car floored the accelerator and caught a glimpse of the Jeep as it dropped into the shadows of an underground parking garage. A quick look at the building explained the unexpected move: the garage belonged to the Le Méridien Montparnasse Hotel, an old, quality establishment in the heart of the upscale Montparnasse district, with over nine hundred rooms and suites, and a reputation for discretion. The visitor took the elevator to reception on the first floor. He registered under a pseudonym, paid cash, and went straight up to Room 2541 with a small suitcase in his hand.

The hotel guest was Atef Bseiso, a round-faced, elegantly

dressed forty-four-year-old Palestinian who had been living in Tunis for the last ten years. He was the Palestine Liberation Organization—the PLO—liaison officer, working with, among others, the French internal security service, the Direction de la Surveillance du Territoire (DST). He was considered a rising star in his organization. His good relations with European intelligence agencies were, in large part, a product of his personal charm and charisma.

Bseiso was drained from the drive—he had covered the six-hundred-mile journey in nine hours flat. Despite his fatigue and the alluring pull of the room's king-size bed, he went to the phone. Bseiso did not want to pass his only night in Paris with a remote control in his hand. He took out an address book and dialed the number of a PLO bodyguard. In Tunis, Bseiso felt safe; in Europe, he feared the Israelis. He had a list of names and numbers of men, frequently unarmed, who would accompany senior PLO officials in Europe to give them a sense of security. He told the man he'd be going out to dinner. The bodyguard offered to pick Bseiso up at the hotel. "I've driven enough for today," Bseiso said. "Let's say nine at the entrance to the hotel. *A tout à l'heure.*" He showered and got dressed.

Shabtai Shavit, the head of Israel's Institute for Intelligence and Special Operations, the Mossad, received a brief message in the operation's war room, located in a safe house in the 11th Arrondissement: "He's in the Méridien Montparnasse. We're getting ready." Shavit leaned back in his chair. The operation was in high gear. Shavit, in his early fifties, had run the Mossad for the past three years, and was well acquainted with undercover operations. He had served for six years as commander of the Mossad's Caesarea unit, which was charged with special operations and with running undercover Mossad combatants in enemy territory. He was in Paris on a borrowed identity: a different name was on the passport in the pocket of his blazer. None of his peers in the French secret service, or any other branch of the French intelligence services, knew he was in the country. His gut told him the mission would go well. He had complete confidence in the professionalism of Caesarea's combatants.

Ilan C, Caesarea's intelligence collection officer, placed the thirty-by-forty-centimeter pictures of the facade of the Méridien Montparnasse Hotel on a table in another room in the Mossad safe house. The new pictures had been shot from a variety of angles and included the streets surrounding the hotel. The surveillance team had taken them as soon as Bseiso checked in. The operational plans, drawn up in advance by Caesarea officers, took a number of hotels into consideration, primarily the Méridien Etoile, an elegant hotel situated a few steps from the Champs-Elysées—but not the Méridien Montparnasse. Bseiso's unexpected choice forced them to revise their plans accordingly. The work was done quickly and efficiently. In less than an hour a new plan was brought before Shavit. Time was tight, and Shavit, never garrulous under even the most relaxed circumstances, kept it brief. He asked Caesarea's commander and the head of the assassination squad a few questions about the operation. He honed a few key points, and then, satisfied, approved the mission.

The surveillance team had followed Bseiso for three days. They tracked him from the moment he arrived in Berlin; his meetings with German intelligence officers of the Bundesamt für Verfassungsschutz (BfV); the purchase of the Jeep; his sprint to Paris. A half-dozen combatants, two cars, and two motorcycles comprised the surveillance team. Throughout, none of the operation's planners at Caesarea had any idea where Bseiso would stay. Would he choose the apartment of a friend, a flat set up by the DST, or a plush hotel room, courtesy of the kingly budget of Fatah, the largest faction of the PLO? Now they knew where they had to act. The operation needed to go into full swing immediately, as Bseiso, a notoriously reluctant traveler, might well spend only one night in Paris. Perhaps the following day, after meeting a colleague from the DST, he would return home, and the opportunity that had presented itself would be gone, possibly forever. Intelligence reports showed that Bseiso, whose job demanded frequent travel, tried to stay in Tunis as much as possible. When he did leave, he flew, a mode of travel not so susceptible to Israeli attack. Planes go directly from point A to point B. The traveler is never alone. People in cars meander, stop for gas, and spend the night at hotels. Bseiso, it turned out, was in fact planning to leave the following evening. He would drive to Marseilles, put the Jeep on a ferry to Tunis, and surprise his wife, Dima, and their three children with the new car.

The Israelis waited in ambush outside the hotel. They assumed Bseiso would go out for dinner. When he returned, tired and contented, they would act. The late hours of the night, when the streets are quiet and empty, were always best for covert operations. The final decision would be in the hands of the two assassins, "Tom" and "Frank." The point man, Tom, would pull the trigger. Up until the last instant, he would have the authority to call off the operation: he would raise his weapon only when certain that his team would emerge unscathed.

Atef Bseiso was a target because of the role he played in the slaughter of eleven Israeli Olympians in Munich, in 1972, almost twenty years prior. Shabtai Shavit wanted him to pay the price for participating in the killings. Prime Minister Yitzhak Shamir authorized the mission and gave it his blessing. The state of Israel was on the verge of closing its case against another one of the "bastards," as they were known in the Mossad, who took part in the Munich Massacre.

Bseiso did go out to dinner. The Caesarea surveillance team shadowed him, undetected, the whole time. They checked that he wasn't being guarded by his DST hosts. Bseiso, his bodyguard, and an unidentified Lebanese woman spent a pleasant night at a Hippopotamus Grill chain restaurant. It was after midnight when Bseiso picked up the tab and went back to the Jeep. He sat in the back, his bodyguard drove, and his friend sat in the front seat. They had a very loud, animated conversation in Arabic. A short drive brought them to the entrance of the Méridien Montparnasse. The Rue du Commandant Mouchotte was quiet; few cars passed by.

Bseiso got out and said goodbye to his friends. He took one step back, preparing to move in the direction of the hotel. A few seconds later, two young men approached him. Their walk was loose, casual. Tom, the point man, raised his hand and pulled the trigger. The Beretta 0.22 issued its shots in silence, the retorts muzzled by a silencer. The three bullets hit Bseiso in the head. He fell on the spot, next to his friend's car, his final inhalation a gurgle. The hot cartridges were caught, along with the clues they held, in a sturdy cloth bag attached to the pistol. Within seconds, the assassin and his backup were rapidly retreating down the street.

"Abie," the commander of the squad, waited for them near the corner, 150 yards away. He watched them cross to the other side of Avenue du Maine and, from the other side of the street, at a more casual pace, watched their backs. This standard procedure was meant to thwart a mishap during the escape phase of a mission—a highly unlikely scenario, since it takes bystanders many long seconds, if not minutes, to realize that an assassination has just taken place. Nonetheless, the possibility couldn't be ignored. Within twenty seconds the point man and his number two were at the corner of a one-way street. According to Mossad procedure, the getaway car always waits two 90-degree turns from the scene of an operation. The pair made a left onto Rue Vandamme, where the waiting car had kept its motor running.

Abie suddenly noticed two figures coming after his men. They were breathing heavily and speaking animatedly. This was a fast-approaching threat; they needed to be stopped. They could not be allowed to turn the corner and see the escape vehicle, or, even worse, commit the license plate to memory. Abie started toward them, his quick pace authoritative and threatening. When he was within fifteen feet of the pair he pulled out his Beretta. Holding it in front of their faces, he shouted: "Stop!" The weapon froze them in their tracks. They put their hands in the air, stumbled backward, turned around, and broke into a run in the direction of the hotel. Abie pocketed his gun and walked down Avenue du Maine. He watched his men turn left onto the narrow street and got into a second car waiting for him on his side of the avenue. He checked his watch: fifty-five seconds had elapsed since the first shot was fired. He smiled to himself. The account was squared; the mission, a success. He pushed a button, sending confirmation to the commander of Caesarea. In less than two hours, the point man, his number two, the squad leader, the commander of Caesarea, his staff officers, and Shabtai Shavit, had all left French soil.

• • •

Brigadier General Azriel Nevo, Prime Minister Yitzhak Shamir's military aide, lay awake in bed waiting for the red, top secret telephone to ring. He picked it up quickly and heard a familiar voice say, "Azriel, it went according to plan." He recognized "Amir," Shabtai Shavit's chief of staff, on the other end of the line.

"Thanks, I'll pass it on."

Nevo sat up in bed and dialed Shamir's number. The prime minister picked up on the first ring. "Mr. Prime Minister, I just got word from Shavit's office, the Paris affair went smoothly."

"Thank you," Shamir said, and hung up.

Nevo put down the phone. Shamir, he thought, had nerves of steel. He and Shavit were two of a kind. Nevo went back to sleep thinking about how *Le Figaro*'s headline might read the next morning.

News of the assassination traveled fast. Some Western media outlets automatically attributed the hit to the Mossad, even pointing to the possibility of revenge for the Munich murders of 1972. The Bseiso family, one of the largest and most respected clans in Gaza City, set up a traditional mourning tent, where they received hundreds of visitors. Bseiso was hailed as a "victim of the Intifada." Yasser Arafat, the founder of Fatah, was in Amman, Jordan, recovering from head injuries sustained when his plane was forced to crash-land in the Libyan desert during a sandstorm earlier that year.

Arafat told dozens of reporters that the Israeli Mossad was responsible for the assassination. "I warned them," he said, "*dir balkum*, be careful, the Mossad will hunt us down one by one, officer by officer. . . . Unfortunately, we have lost a national hero."

Israeli authorities never issued an official response. One of Prime Minister Shamir's spokespersons told *The New York Times* that the accusation was "totally and completely ridiculous." The head of Military Intelligence, Major General Uri Saguy, responded to Arafat's claims with an unperturbed: "*Nu,* so Arafat says we did it, *hat ehr gezukt*" (Yiddish for: He says so, so what?).

Officers at the Mossad's Brussels station were shocked. "Eyal," a high-ranking officer in Caesarea, hurried up the stairs to see "Haggai," his superior.

"Didn't we take this guy off the list?" Eyal asked.

"We took him off. I don't know what's going on." Haggai shrugged.

Both of them knew the deceased. Back in 1988, the two of them, in previous posts as officers at Mossad headquarters in Tel Aviv, had erased his name from the Mossad hit list. The removal had gone through all the proper channels. Nahum Admoni, the head of the Mossad at the time, had approved the move. Yet someone had put Bseiso back on the list and then led a covert operation to kill him on French soil. That someone was none other than Shabtai Shavit—a brilliant tactician and professional, who had excelled at every post he held along the chain of command, and who had the ear and the confidence of every prime minister he worked under.

Early in 1992, Shavit called a former protégé, the current head of Caesarea, to a short meeting. He asked him to check which of the terrorists involved in the Munich attack were still alive. Shavit was old-school, one of those who refused to close the book on Munich. As far as he was concerned, the state of Israel had painted a well-deserved target on the faces of everyone involved in the planning or the execution of the massacre. They

would all pay with their lives; when and where was of no conse-
quence. Mossad combatants were charged with carrying out the
assassination orders, which had been passed down from Golda
Meir to each successive prime minister.

Shavit believed in Israel's responsibility to its citizens, at home
and abroad—he believed in the necessity of fulfilling this executive order not just because he saw it as moral and just, but because he knew that no one else would carry it out in his place. He
would do all in his power to see the mission through.

A few months after the assassination, Shavit was officially invited to meet the newly appointed head of the DST. Forgoing
pleasantries, the French intelligence officer fired his opening vol-
ley: "We know you killed Bseiso. We're still working on the
proof. When it comes through, you'll get what's coming to you.
In no way am I willing to allow you to turn Paris into your stage
for acts of war and assassinations. We're not going back to the
early seventies, when you did whatever the hell you wanted here.
I will not allow it to happen," he said, pounding his fist on the
table.

Shavit was impassive. "Point taken," he said coolly, running
his hand through his thinning, slicked-back hair, and then sipping
from an espresso he'd been served earlier. Shavit knew there was
no chance the French would find anything that would tie Israel to
the assassination. The mission had gone without a hitch. Without
a flicker of emotion he bid his colleague farewell, and left the office of the chief commander of the DST.

The Israeli action could not go unpunished; it was a sharp embarrassment, a stinging slap in the face to the French government. The Mossad is convinced that the French responded by
deliberately leaking the name of a high-ranking Palestinian
source in Arafat's Tunis office. The agent, Adnan Yassin, had
been working for the Mossad for years, informing them of all
that transpired in the office and among the Diaspora Palestinian

leadership. In October 1993, Yassin was arrested, and never heard from again. In addition, the French alerted the Palestinians to the presence of Mossad listening devices that had been placed in antique French furniture the PLO had received as a gift from Yassin. The French retribution handicapped Israel during the sensitive negotiations leading up to the Oslo Accords in 1993.

. . .

Three different, but often intertwined, factors come into play when a state decides to carry out an assassination—prevention, deterrence, and revenge. The role of prevention is clear—killing a known terrorist can prevent the next attack, most demonstrably in the case of an imminent "ticking bomb." And in certain instances, the well-timed assassination of a terrorist leader can seriously wound an organization, hindering its ability to function indefinitely.

Deterrence is a more complex factor. Essentially, its goal is to violently persuade those considering a career in terrorism to choose a different vocation. Undoubtedly some do. "We'll never know how many," a former high-ranking Mossad officer told me, smiling contentedly. True, but the ultimate effectiveness of deterrence-by-assassination is open to question.

Deterrence is often woven together with the third factor, revenge and punishment. The aim here is to make it clear that he who hurts us, as an organization, as a people, will forever walk around in fear of a sudden, unprepared-for death. But there is an added tactical value: terrorists who are constantly looking over their shoulder in fear for their lives are less preoccupied with executing terror.

Decision makers and heads of intelligence services the world over will vehemently deny succumbing to revenge's ancient allure, with its biblical demand for an eye for an eye, a tooth for a tooth. Yet revenge, to differing degrees, has played a role in each and every assassination carried out in Israel's name, throughout its history. The same can be said for democracies like Britain, France, and the United States. Usually, "revenge" is not spoken of openly. Different, softer words are used, words that people can live with; phrases like "closing the circle."

Revenge and punishment are part of a government's decision-making process. For instance, the ongoing hunt for Osama Bin Laden. To what degree is the search for the 9/11 mastermind based on the need for prevention or deterrence? Now that numerous Bin Laden clones have arisen, to what extent is the hunt driven by a desire for revenge and punishment?

In the case of Atef Bseiso, revenge was served cold, twenty years after the crime. Bseiso joined a list of more than a dozen people killed by Israel in the wake of the Munich attack. Bseiso, the last of them, closed the circle.

2   A YEAR OF TERROR

Terrorism hit an awful peak in 1972. Palestinian groups, frustrated by their failure to execute attacks against Israel from the Occupied Territories of the West Bank and the Gaza Strip, exported their activities beyond the boundaries of the Middle East. Throughout 1972, a record number of high-profile attacks were carried out against Israelis and Jews. The Palestinians' daring offensive incorporated many forms of violence. They hijacked planes, assassinated Israeli diplomats, and sent letter bombs all across the European continent. As a result of their actions, the plight of the Palestinian people began to seep into the world's collective consciousness. Terrorism—their chosen method—was proving successful. Each deadly attack raised the ante. Operations grew bolder, more sophisticated, more theatrical.

• • •

On May 8, 1972, Belgian Sabena Flight 571 was en route from Brussels, via Vienna, to Tel Aviv. On board were ten crew members and ninety passengers, sixty-seven of them Jewish. Also on board were four members of Black September, an amorphous branch of Fatah. The terrorists (two men and two women) were armed with hand grenades, a revolver, and two five-pound explosive devices. In the late afternoon, as the plane flew over the Greek island of Rhodes, the commander of the terrorist cell quietly made his way to the pilot's wide-open cabin door. He pulled out a loaded gun and ordered the pilot to land the plane in Tel Aviv—a wildly daring move, considering that Israel's premier counterterrorist unit, Sayeret Matkal, was five miles from Israel's international airport. The terrorist grabbed the PA system and introduced himself: "This is Captain Kamal Rifa'at, your new captain. . . ."

In a quick phone consultation, Defense Minister Moshe Dayan, the hero of the 1967 Six Day War, and Golda Meir, prime minister, decided to allow the aircraft to land at Lod International Airport. It touched down and was immediately escorted to the far end of the tarmac. Within hours, top military brass convened at the airport terminal. Defense Minister Dayan and Transportation Minister Shimon Peres were joined by Israeli Defense Forces chief of staff Lieutenant General David Elazar and several other IDF generals, including the head of Military Intelligence, Major General Aharon Yariv, and Major General Ariel Sharon (who later served as defense minister and, from 2001, as prime minister). Dayan directed Victor Cohen, head of the interrogation branch of the Shabak, Israel's internal secret service, to conduct spurious negotiations with the terrorists. Dayan and Meir had no intention of yielding to their extortionate demands—to free 315 convicted Palestinian terrorists imprisoned in Israeli jails—Dayan just wanted to deprive the terrorists of sleep.

Next, Dayan summoned Sayeret Matkal, Israel's elite antiterror unit, commanded by Ehud Barak. (In twenty-seven years

Barak too would become prime minister.) Dayan instructed the unit to cripple the plane and rescue the hostages. Shortly thereafter, Barak and his officers began to practice storming an identical Boeing 707 on a nearby runway on the far side of the airport, while mechanics were rendering the hijacked plane unable to fly.

Victor Cohen's negotiations, conducted over the plane's radio system, kept the hijackers up all night, as they reiterated their demand that Israel open the gates of its prisons. On May 9, at 0900 hours, after more than ten hours of continuous negotiations, Cohen succeeded in convincing Rifa'at to send the pilot out with a sample of their explosives, to show to the Israelis. Cohen was playing the good cop as he argued that he needed to convince the one-eyed defense minister Dayan—that feared warrior—how lethal Black September's intentions in fact were. Pilot Reginald Levy, traveling to Israel to celebrate his fiftieth birthday together with his wife, provided Israel's security forces with critical details: the number of hijackers, their physical appearance, the contours of the black packages—probably explosive devices—they clutched. He confirmed that there were no seats next to the emergency exits of the plane, a matter of supreme importance to Barak and his staff officers, who knew that success hinged on surprise and speed. Levy returned to the hijackers and reported that Dayan had agreed to their terms. The 315 Palestinian prisoners would be delivered to the airport, and from there sent on to Cairo. Flight 571 would meet them in the Egyptian capital and the hostages would be freed. First, a technical team of mechanics would repair the aircraft.

Sixteen commandos from Sayeret Matkal, dressed as El Al mechanics in white jumpsuits, approached the plane. They gathered near the emergency exits of the aircraft and along the wings and, in a synchronized assault, burst inside. They immediately killed the two male hijackers and apprehended the two females, inadvertently killing one hostage in the process. The Israeli commandos had taken control of the plane in ninety seconds. The astonishing operation, the first of its kind, soon echoed around the world. A wave of pride washed over Israel. Israeli ingenuity, many felt, could conquer all.

That feeling didn't change, even though three weeks after the Sabena mission a devastating attack occurred at Israel's Lod Airport. Three men, members of the Japanese Red Army, a Marxist terrorist group, had volunteered to act under the auspices of the left-wing terror organization the Popular Front for the Liberation of Palestine (PFLP), and carry out the attack. Their goal: to murder as many people as possible, thereby garnering maximum worldwide exposure. They arrived in Israel on an Air France flight from Paris. They went through passport control, claimed their bags, and withdrew AK-47 assault rifles and grenades. Then they opened fire and lobbed hand grenades at the dense crowd waiting nearby. In the chaos that ensued, two of the attackers were killed, probably by one of their own grenades. The third terrorist, Kozo Okamoto, fled. He made it to the tarmac and was captured alive. (He would be sentenced to life behind bars, but was released fourteen years later as part of a prisoner exchange.) Okamoto and his accomplices killed twenty-four people and injured seventy-two. Several of the victims were Puerto Rican pilgrims.

• • •

As the pitiless campaign waged by Palestinian terrorists against the state of Israel unfolded, it exerted a far-reaching influence on the development of terrorism worldwide. International terrorist organizations such as the Japanese Red Army, Baader-Meinhof, and the Armenian ASALA watched and learned as the Palestinians expanded the repertoire of murder, attempting previously undreamt-of missions. And the Palestinian mastery of terror's twin purposes—propaganda and fear—helped lodge their stateless predicament in the minds of world leaders.

But the worst was yet to come. The failure of the Sabena hijacking increased the resolve of Black September's leadership. They were determined to pull off an unprecedented, earth-shaking attack—a theater of terror that would burn itself into the world's collective consciousness for generations. They chose the Munich Olympics, to be held in August and September of 1972, as their grand stage.

3 NO WARNING BELLS

Shmuel Lalkin, head of the Israeli Olympic Delegation, signed
the letter, sealed it in an envelope, and dropped it in the outgoing
mail pile.

Security and anti-terror precautions were not part of his job
description, but they were important to the former Israeli Defense Forces major. Lalkin stuck out in a crowd: he was tall,
forty-five years old, had broad shoulders and an athletic bounce
to his step, a remnant of his days as a basketball and volleyball
player. His hair was swept back and his mustache, a trademark of
sorts, was always in perfect order. At first glance he seemed hard,
unapproachable. But to those close to him, he was an easygoing
family man, a sports lover who was always quick with a smile.

Lalkin slid back in his chair and looked at the envelope. The
official letter was addressed to the chief security officer of the Education, Culture and Sports Ministry in Jerusalem. In it, Lalkin,
a man who had paid attention to details his entire life, had carefully laid out all his concerns about the security arrangements for
the 20th Olympic Games, to be held in six weeks' time, in Mu-

nich, West Germany. Chief among them, Lalkin emphasized how dangerous it was to place the Israeli team on the ground floor of a dormitory in Munich, accessible to all. He assumed German authorities were handling Olympic security, which made the obvious breach all the more egregious.

Three weeks earlier Lalkin had returned from a seven-day visit to northern Munich, where the finishing touches were being put on the new Olympic Village. While he was there, he inspected the arenas, courts, athletic facilities, and dorms his Olympians would use. Other delegation heads were doing the same. In his notebook Lalkin sketched each and every facility the delegation might need. He planned to relay all relevant information to the athletes and coaches before they took off for Munich, as this would help prepare them for the competitions to come. He recognized the psychological importance of familiarity, the edge, however small, it might grant his athletes. Appraising security arrangements was far from his mind.

His priorities shifted when Walter Troeger, mayor of the Olympic Village, gave him a tour of the Israeli dorms at 31 Connollystrasse. The ground-floor location, insecure, vulnerable, made him uncomfortable. In Lalkin's mind there was simply no defensible logic to support the decision to place the Israelis at street level. He asked to meet with an Olympic security official. West German representatives from the International Olympic Committee were quick to arrange a meeting with an officer named Ruprecht from the Munich police department. Lalkin explained that he bore no official security position but that certain points had come to light and he wished to review some of the security precautions in place for the Israeli delegation. Ruprecht listened in silence. When Lalkin was through, Ruprecht attempted to ease his mind, telling him that he would put the Israeli dorms under tighter security and heavier surveillance. Lalkin wasn't satisfied. He asked whether the Israeli athletes could be moved to a more secure building, with higher floors, where the entrances could be properly supervised. "Sir," Ruprecht responded, "I don't think it's any of your business. All our decisions concerning your delegation's living quarters have been coordinated with your embassy's security people and the Israeli Olympic Committee. Our decisions were made together." Lalkin left the room in silence, hanging his head.

Back in Israel Lalkin was unsure how to act. The security issues continued to gnaw at him; his sleep was fitful. Eventually, he decided to call two friends, men he'd known in the pre-state Palmach fighting unit and later in the IDF, and who were now members of the Shabak. They directed him to Arie Shumar, the Education, Culture and Sports Ministry's chief security officer. It was Shumar to whom Lalkin sent his official letter, outlining his concerns. "I didn't feel comfortable with the security arrangements for our athletes. It was important to me to let people know that I thought things should be done differently," he would later tell the prime minister's official investigative committee, whose top secret report was made public for the first time as a result of the research for this book. In their findings, known as the Kopel Report, the three-member committee found that several Israeli officials had been given the opportunity to choose the location of the team's dorms, perhaps in an area easily supervised or on one of the top floors, but hadn't done so. Not one Israeli official, and many were contacted, asked to change the Israeli location in the village.

The response to Lalkin's letter came in a plain brown envelope. "Dear Mr. Lalkin: As Manager of the Israeli Olympic team it would be advisable for you to concentrate on sports. Leave security to the security personnel. Yours Truly, Arie Shumar, Chief Security Officer, Education, Culture and Sports Ministry." The few, arrogant lines ignored Lalkin's warnings. He had a premonition, he knew the Israeli athletes were at risk, but it wasn't enough to change the thinking of the entire defense establishment.

What Lalkin didn't know was that the Israeli defense establishment was doing nothing to protect the country's Olympians. Everything concerning the protection of the Olympic delegation (and other Israeli national groups) was falling through the cracks. No senior official felt any need to address the issue. Israel, at the time, was under mounting stress: planes were hijacked, Israeli officials targeted. The attacks were coming in quick succession, but the Shabak, the organization charged with homeland security, failed to connect any of the dots. Their failure went far beyond ignoring the security flaws in the Olympic Village. The deeper, more basic failure was rooted in a lack of interest, a downright disregard for a rapidly escalating situation. Only bloodshed would facilitate real change.

While Lalkin worried, at Mossad headquarters, in the Hadar Dafna building at 39–41 King Saul Boulevard in north Tel Aviv, no one was losing any sleep. Work flowed in and out of the cold concrete building as usual. Even three hundred yards away at the IDF's headquarters, on the south side of King Saul Boulevard, where Branch 4's crude wooden cabins were located, there was no new activity. Branch 4 of Military Intelligence, charged with collecting, analyzing, and assessing data on Palestinian terror organizations, did not earmark a single piece of data relating to the possibility of an Olympic attack. The Kopel Report examined the intelligence agencies' conduct in the prelude to the Olympics and revealed, "The Defense Establishment continually received information on the express desire to commit an attack in Europe. The flow of information was thin in comparison with other times during the year, but in August 1972 there was a rise in the number of reports regarding a planned attack in Europe. None mentioned the Olympics by name." One report from that time did mention an "international event," which might have hinted at the terrorist leaders' intentions to carry out a high-profile attack, but it received no special attention.

Even on Thursday, August 31, the sixth day of the Games, when the heads of Military Intelligence, the Shabak, and the Mossad met for their weekly conference, no bells were sounded. The committee analyzed the week's intelligence reports, but failed to associate anything with the ongoing Games. Intelligence officers who later went over the information that existed at the time had this to say: "Do you have any idea how many bits of intelligence we get that relate to future 'international events' and then result in nothing? On the basis of that type of intelligence you cannot issue an official warning."

4 THE GAMES OF PEACE AND JOY

The opening ceremony of the 20th Olympic Games was dazzling. A record 121 delegations and over seven thousand athletes entered the stadium in dress uniforms, took their places on the well-groomed grass, and watched as whip-wielding Bavarian dancers twirled and stomped. Thousands of doves fluttered skyward. An eighteen-year-old German athlete, Günter Zahn, ran into the stadium, bounded up the steps, and lit the Olympic torch. The Games were under way.

The positive feeling in the stadium was carefully constructed to erase the scars of Germany's bloody past. Local organizers did everything they could to convey the message that Germany's rehabilitation was complete, that 1936—when Berlin, under Adolf Hitler, hosted the 11th Olympiad against a backdrop of discrimination and violence—was a relic of a dead past. Federal officials, the local Bavarian state government, German Olympic officials, the police, the press, and ordinary citizens were all part of an effort to showcase a progressive, an enlightened, a cultured Germany.

The Israeli delegation's participation in these Olympics was central to Germany's theatrical act of repudiation. Israel's twenty-seven-member squad was that country's largest ever. Henry Hershkowitz, a marksman, carried the blue and white flag through the stadium, trembling with excitement. "I felt awesome pride that Jews could raise their flag on German soil," he told reporters after the event. "This is proof that the Nazis weren't able to crush the Jewish spirit, the Israeli spirit." An especially loud roar engulfed the Israeli team as it entered the packed stadium.

Over four thousand reporters, editorialists, and radio broadcasters were in attendance to cover the games—more evidence of Germany's desire to be seen as a new country. About two thousand television reporters and crew were by their side. These numbers far exceeded those of the 1968 Mexico City Games—indeed of any previous Olympics. The main events would draw a billion viewers in over one hundred countries.

The live broadcast was one of the great achievements of the 20th Olympic Games. In today's world, where a cell phone can take pictures, record sound, and serve as a fully functioning computer, a live broadcast might seem trivial, but in 1972 it was a technological wonder. The Munich Olympics would dominate the international airwaves. No war or major geopolitical conflict was going on; there was nothing that could compete with the Games. The Germans planned to squeeze every possible ounce of positive publicity they could out of the seventeen-day event.

From the outset, the Germans emphasized the Olympic message of world peace. They didn't want the world to see them holding guns, which might evoke old images. No armed guards or police were positioned in the Olympic Village or at stadium entrances. Instead, two thousand Olys, ushers in sky-blue uniforms, were given the twin duties of perimeter security and traffic control. Only those with a pass could enter the fenced village. But as the Games progressed, the ushers' diligence waned. The perimeter fence added little additional security: many of the Olympians hopped it with ease, well after midnight, on their way back from Munich's beer halls.

Security costs for the Games came to $2 million. The relatively insignificant sum was not born of miserliness, but of a frank desire to keep security to a minimum. For subsequent Olympics, security costs rose exponentially, peaking in 2004 at $1 billion. The German security concept, one that held that guards, both visible and undercover, could only tarnish the Games and blacken the image of the new Germany they were trying to convey, unknowingly facilitated Black September's plans. German authorities were well equipped to deal with unruly men and copious quantities of beer, but were utterly unprepared for a terrorist attack.

• • •

The Israeli delegation set out for Munich on the 21st of August. No security detail, covert or otherwise, accompanied them. Several days before their departure the delegation had been invited to the Wingate Institute, Israel's National Center for Physical Education and Sports, for a standard briefing. Arie Shumar, the Education, Culture and Sports Ministry's chief security officer, gave the address, which seemed brief and banal to the Israelis. They had heard the same advice each time they left the country to represent Israel. Don't draw attention to yourselves. No loud conversations in Hebrew, no clothing with obvious Hebrew symbols. Beware of suspicious packages in your dorms. Avoid opening any type of mail, even if it comes from home.

There was no mention of a possible mega-attack in the briefing. Complacency? The mere appearance of control and order? Yes, that was how things were on the Israeli side.

Most of the Israeli delegation was housed at 31 Connollystrasse, along with the Uruguayan and Hong Kong teams. Security conditions in the dorms left the athletes ill at ease. The top secret Kopel Report states on page nine, "The testimony of athletes, delegation leaders, journalists and television crews makes clear that members of the delegation, other officials, and family members frequently talked among themselves about the obvious lack of security in the village, particularly regarding their housing. The uncomfortable feeling intensified as the alacrity of the security ushers abated. The proximity of the Sudanese team's dorms and the ubiquity of Palestinian workers in the village intensified the general discomfort. Many of the athletes feared they would be attacked during their events. No one considered the possibility of a hostage situation. The fears festering in the minds of the athletes didn't result in a call to bolster security. They didn't act, they said, because they assumed that the security forces must be working undercover." These words do not begin to convey the scandalous enormity of the German, and Israeli, security lapses in Munich.

On August 23, the chief security officer of the Israeli embassy in Bonn arrived in Munich to inspect the security arrangements—

of the Israeli television crews. He met with Lalkin and the head of the Israeli Olympic Committee about "routine security matters," according to the Kopel Report. Lalkin's premonition—that his team was in danger—was stronger than ever. He requested a sidearm. The security officer refused.

5 | THE MISSION UNFOLDS

A middle-aged couple waited for their four pieces of luggage to arrive. The man, dressed in a well-tailored suit, hoisted the bags onto two carts. They joined the flow of people walking toward the customs line and the exit beyond.

The Palestinian man worked as a *saya'an* (a Hebrew security term meaning "helper"—an uninformed, ideologically motivated accomplice) for Fatah and its Black September wing in Europe. The "wife," another *saya'an,* joined him to lend legitimacy to their cover. The Fatah planners knew that an Arab man, traveling alone, to a city hosting the Olympics, with four bulging suitcases in tow, might raise the suspicions of even the most soporific customs official, putting the entire mission at risk.

The couple had almost made it through customs when an officer beckoned them aside. The couple pressed together and nervously made their way to the inspection platform. They presented North African passports and were asked to open their identical bags. The husband refused. He began to yell and scream. He was a businessman, not a criminal. He had never been so thoroughly embarrassed in all his travels throughout Europe. Why should he be treated this way? The bored customs officers looked on, eyes half-closed. They had seen this act before, and they knew how it ended—the traveler opened his bags for inspection, end of story. Those who yelled the loudest were often the guiltiest. They had seen plenty of drugs and gold cross their path.

After yelling for several minutes, the Palestinian lowered his voice and asked the customs officer which bag he should open. The officer picked one. After wiping the sweat from his brow and fiddling for his keys, the man opened the suitcase. The release of the locks popped the lid. Lingerie, in many colors and styles, swamped the inspection desk. The officer motioned to the man: close your case and carry on. He didn't ask the couple to open their other three pieces of luggage. Eight AK-47s, dozens of magazines loaded with 7.62mm bullets, and ten grenades slid by undetected on the wobbly wheels of a trolley.

The couple left the terminal, rented a roomy car, and drove the 280 miles to Munich. They had no idea what they were transporting or why. They were couriers. Now and again they were told to carry suitcases, letters, and packages. They never asked questions, and had never been caught.

On arriving in Munich, they followed their instructions to the letter. The couple placed their suitcases in four different lockers in the Munich central railway station and handed the keys over to the concierge of a small, nearby hotel. Hours later, a Black September commander came by the front desk and picked up his package.

The senior members of Fatah, working under the name Black September, sighed in collective relief when they learned that the baggage had safely arrived. The operation was on track, progressing exactly as planned. They had thirteen more days. They'd act on the tenth day of the Olympics, in the early morning hours of Tuesday, September 5, 1972.

• • •

Black September was unveiled in the fall of 1971. It was born on the heels of a massacre. In mid-September 1970, King Hussein, the ruler of Jordan, had his back against the wall. Palestinians, who by that time represented nearly 60 percent of the Jordanian population, were on the brink of toppling his regime. Bloody battles erupted in the streets of the capital, Amman. Thousands of Palestinians were slaughtered by Hussein's army. The surviving activists, overpowered, fled for their lives. Thousands entered Syria and from there continued on to the neighborhoods surrounding the Lebanese capital of Beirut. Once there, they began to rebuild their terrorist infrastructure.

Black September's primary mission was to avenge the killings committed by Hussein's Hashemite regime. Its first undertaking was the assassination of Wasfi Al-Tell, the Jordanian prime minister—a man they saw as a sworn enemy of the Palestinians. Al-Tell was gunned down in the Cairo Sheraton on November 27, 1971. One of his killers bent down and, to the astonishment of eyewitnesses, lapped up Al-Tell's blood.

The murder of the prime minister was the first of a slew of revenge killings. Black September operatives, acting in Europe, detonated bombs in the Jordanian embassy in Geneva, lobbed Molotov cocktails at the embassy in Paris, and fired a machine gun at the ambassador to England.

Black September was different from other Palestinian terror organizations: it had no offices, no addresses, no official leaders, and no spokespersons. Fatah members embraced the secrecy surrounding Black September, feeding its aura of mystery, its martial might and propaganda potential. But Black September was not as autonomous as it seemed—Salah Khalaf, widely known as Abu-Iyad, deputy of Arafat and one of the commanders of the Fatah, was Black September's unofficial leader.

Black September's goals were far more than simply revenge. Arafat and other Fatah leaders wanted to demonstrate their power and display—in no uncertain terms—their international prominence after their defeat at the hands of the Jordanians. Fatah leaders also made a strategic decision to become involved in international terrorism, particularly in Europe, where left-wing factions of the Palestinian resistance were hijacking planes and pulling off many different high-profile terrorist stunts, their popularity growing across the Middle East and indeed around the world as a result.

Abu-Iyad never acknowledged his leadership of Black September; he, like Arafat, disavowed any connection to the group. Arafat, when asked about his relationship to Black September at the time, offered this: "We don't know anything about this organization nor are we involved in any of its activities, but we do understand the mentality of young people who are willing to die for the life of Palestine." The technical arrangement whereby Fatah would quietly take the credit for, and publicly disavow any connection to, terror attacks, suited Arafat: it allowed him to build a facade of respectability as head of an organization with clean hands and legitimate, nationalistic aspirations—while approving sensationalistic attacks behind the scenes.

Black September disseminated information on a need-to-know basis. Beyond Abu-Iyad, few were allowed to see the complete picture. Its structure consisted of two inner circles. The first was comprised of Abu-Iyad's disciples. Mohammed Oudeh, an operations officer known as Abu-Daoud, was the most senior. He was the architect of the Munich operation. Fakhri Al-Omri, the operations officer and a rising star in Fatah, served as Abu-Iyad's confidant and right-hand man. Al-Omri was cunning, calm under duress, a gifted tactician, and a skilled organizer. It was he who picked up the keys and collected the weapons from the lockers in Munich, and he followed the operation through all its stages. The other men in this innermost circle were Amin Al-Hindi, who later ran an intelligence wing in the Palestinian Authority, and Atef Bseiso, later Fatah's liaison with European intelligence organizations.

A second circle consisted of accomplices who, like the couple that smuggled in the four suitcases, knew nothing beyond their personal assignments. They handled forged passports, rented cars and apartments, bought plane tickets, and concealed documents. Many were Palestinians living in Europe. Some were university students, others were part of the Palestinian Diaspora who had settled comfortably in Europe, perhaps married locally, while remaining ardent in their desire to help liberate their stolen homeland from the Zionist oppressor. Close to one hundred people of this sort were in Black September's employ.

• • •

The Mossad was caught off guard by the scope of Black September's ambition. Up until May 1972 all the group's operations were aimed at Jordanian targets. The Mossad frequently reported to Prime Minister Meir's cabinet that Black September was interested only in harming the kingdom next door. That argument collapsed on May 8, 1972, when Black September took credit for hijacking Sabena Flight 571. Not only was there no warning of the attack, but the Mossad and Military Intelligence utterly failed to recognize what was clearly a strategic shift: a newfound focus on Israeli targets. Even after Sabena, Israeli intelligence agencies continued to insist that Israel was not the main target; the Sabena highjacking was just a ricochet, the price of proximity to Jordan.

Why did Abu-Iyad choose the Munich Games as the target for a major terror attack? In his book, *Stateless*, Abu-Iyad later wrote that the operation sought to achieve three goals. One was "to present the existence of the Palestinian People to the whole world, whether they like it or not." Another was "to secure the release of 200 Palestinian fighters locked in Israeli jails."

And the third, in a neat encapsulation of the rationale of all terrorists, was this: "to use the unprecedented number of media outlets in one city to display the Palestinian struggle—for better or worse!"

6   SEIZING THE ATHLETES

The bus was filled with the sounds of backslapping and laughter. The jubilant Israeli athletes were on their way back to the Olympic Village after an evening at the theater. The delegation had just seen *Fiddler on the Roof*, in German, with Shmuel Rodensky, the noted Israeli stage actor, in the lead role. He invited the team backstage during the intermission to meet the cast. They took a group picture: their last.

Shmuel Lalkin, head of the delegation, sat at the front of the bus, his wife, Yardena, by his side. Arik, his thirteen-year-old son, was hanging out in the back row with the wrestlers and weight lifters. Yossef Romano, David Berger, Mark Slavin, and Eliezer Halfin were crazy about the kid.

As the bus approached the Olympic Village, Arik sidled up to his father and asked to sleep in the wrestlers' room. Lalkin refused. His family was not part of the delegation, which meant they slept outside of the village, at their own expense. Arik cried and begged. "Dad, c'mon, I'm a big kid already. They're my friends. Just one night." Lalkin did not cave in. He needed to set a personal example for everyone else on the squad. Romano and Halfin came to help Arik out. "We'll look out for him, Shmuel, don't worry, it's only one night. Look how badly he wants to come and, anyway, it'll just keep us loose." Lalkin wouldn't budge. Even a stern look from Yardena didn't change his mind. Principles were immovable, always. Romano, Israel's champion weight lifter in the middleweight class for the last ten years, kept the pressure on for a few more seconds and then returned with Halfin to his seat. At 0030 hours the athletes filed off the bus at the Olympic Village. Yardena and Arik continued on to their apartment, ten minutes away. The pleasant Munich weather brought a few of the Israeli athletes to the dining room for a late night snack. Eventually everybody said good night and went to their quarters.

The delegation had been assigned five apartments. Apartment 1 was for the coaches and judges; Apartment 2, the marksmen, the fencers, and the track and field athletes; Apartment 3, the weight lifters and wrestlers; Apartment 4, the doctor; Apartment 5, Shmuel Lalkin. The women stayed in separate dorms far from the men's quarters. Israel's two sailors were housed in northern Germany, in Kiel, where their competition was being held.

It was almost one in the morning when Lalkin finally went to his room. He set his alarm for 6 A.M. He wanted to support Mark Slavin, the rookie wrestler, by attending his pre-match weigh-in.

While the members of the Israeli delegation were enjoying *Fiddler on the Roof,* eight Palestinian terrorists, traveling solo and in pairs, arrived at the Munich central railway station, just a ten-minute walk from the theater, and ordered dinner. They were excited. Nobody could sit still. Whispers were exchanged. This was their first face-to-face meeting. Seated around a rectangular table, they learned the particulars of the mission. One of the commanders leaned in from the head of the table and, speaking in a hushed tone, explained that they were going to kidnap the Israeli athletes in the Olympic Village, take them hostage, and release them in exchange for over two hundred Palestinian prisoners held behind bars in Israel. The hostages and the kidnappers would fly to an Arab state, where the exchange would be made. The operation, called Ikrit and Biram, was named in memory of two Christian villages near the Israeli border with Lebanon. The villagers were forcibly evacuated by the Israelis in 1951 "until the security situation allows their return." Abu-Iyad chose the code name as a symbol of the Palestinian desire to return to a homeland that had been torn away from under their feet.

Jamal Al-Jishey, a dark-skinned nineteen-year-old, was brimming with motivation. Years later, as one of the three Palestinians to live through Munich, he would say (as captured in the documentary film *One Day in September*), "I felt great pride and happiness that I would be participating in an operation against the Israelis. I was finally going to fulfill my dream." Just a few months before, as the heat of the summer started to rise, Al-Jishey was summoned to an elite training camp established by Fatah leaders on the Mediterranean shore, a few miles south of Beirut. The Al-Jisheys lived in Shatila, the teeming Palestinian refugee camp in Beirut. Fifty men, the youngest of them only seventeen, arrived with Al-Jishey for basic training. All the recruits learned how to fire an AK-47 assault rifle and properly release F-1 hand grenades. At the end of the training session, six out of the fifty were selected. They lived in Palestinian refugee camps in Lebanon, and were ready to give their lives if necessary.

The group's members were: Adnan Al-Jishey, twenty-six, uncle of Jamal Al-Jishey, married, and a gifted student who held a chemistry scholarship to the American University of Beirut; Mohammed Safady, nineteen, garrulous and confident; Khalid Jawad, a strong soccer player who had lived in West Germany for two years; Ahmed Sheik Thaa, who grew up in Germany; and Afif Ahmed Hamid, a veteran member of the Fatah organization who had recently returned to Beirut after studying for a little more than a year at a German university.

The six were told that they had been selected for a top secret mission. The details of the operation remained a mystery. They were instructed to leave their families without telling them anything about what they were doing. In mid-July, the month before the Olympics, the group of six flew to Libya for advanced military training. In the isolation of the desert camp the six young men became one cohesive group. "We got to know each other during training in Libya; we were all alike, children of the Palestinian refugee camps with a shared cause and a shared aim," Jamal Al-Jishey said. Al-Jishey and his partners endured endless hours of intensive training drills at a tent camp deep in the heart of the Libyan desert. In the dead heat of July, an exhaustive exercise routine beat them into shape. Their daily regimen included endless sprints and leaps, especially over walls and fences. Al-Jishey was sure he was going to be sent into a Zionist army base. He never imagined that the drills were preparing him for quick entry into the Olympic Village in Munich, Germany.

Muhammad Massalha, twenty-seven, was appointed commander of the operation. He spoke fluent German. As a teen, he had lived in West Germany for several years. He chose the nickname Issa, Arabic for Jesus. His second in command, Tony (Yussef

Nazzal), used the nom de guerre Che Guevara, in tribute to the South American revolutionary. Abu-Iyad referred to Tony as the military mind behind Ikrit and Biram. He was a well-educated twenty-five-year-old who spoke German well. Both men were brought into the limited circle of knowledge. In early summer, Issa and Tony visited Munich. They watched the village being built, learning its layout and its points of vulnerability. Palestinian accomplices, many of them students at German universities, helped Issa and Tony collect information. They did not ask the goal of the mission. Their mantra was blind, unflinching assistance.

With the weapons safely stored in the train station lockers, the leaders of the operation, Abu-Iyad, Abu-Daoud, and Fakhri Al-Omri, had to see to the safe arrival of the six terrorists. It was their duty to ensure that the foot soldiers, without whom the meticulously planned operation would have to be aborted, would fly out of Tripoli and arrive in Munich without arousing suspicion. There was the constant threat of discovery; one alert customs official could bring the whole mission to a halt. That did not happen.

On August 31, five days into the Olympic Games, Jamal Al-Jishey, his uncle Adnan, and Mohammed Safady landed in Munich. The three flew from Tripoli, and stopped briefly in Rome before landing in Munich. The other three foot soldiers arrived in Munich via Belgrade. They each held a Jordanian passport, forged in Beirut and delivered to Tripoli. Each passport had a fake West German entry visa. The work was so amateurish that in one of the passports the visa was attached upside down, crossed out with a black X, and replaced by an additional visa, placed right side up, on the next page. The two groups were met by Issa and Tony and taken to several small hotels and hostels located in the city center, next to the train station. During the following four days, the eight Palestinians acted like normal tourists, sightseeing, eating out, and catching up on sleep. Jamal Al-Jishey even went to two Olympic volleyball games.

On September 4, shortly before midnight, the group of eight met at the central railway station restaurant, where they learned what their mission entailed. After settling the bill, the group walked over to the nearby lockers to collect the weapons that had been waiting for them all week. They returned to their separate hotels and changed into red training suits, which would help them blend in with the athletes in the Olympic Village. They rode in two cabs. Jamal Al-Jishey, the only one to speak publicly about that night, said, "I was young, full of enthusiasm and drive, and the idea of Palestine and returning there was all that controlled my thinking and my being. We knew that achieving our objective would cost lives, but since the day we joined up, we had been aware that there was a possibility of martyrdom at any time in the name of Palestine. We were not afraid, but we felt the appre- hension that a person feels when embarking on an important mission, the fear of failure."

At 0410 hours, two groups of four operatives each reached the village's perimeter fence, near Gate 25A. They aroused no suspi- cion. Like many of the athletes returning from a night on the town, they wore Olympic sweat suits and were ostensibly sneak- ing back to their rooms. One of the two terrorist bands met a group of American athletes near the fence. The tipsy Americans and the wired Palestinians helped each other over the simple, six- foot barrier. Once inside the village the two groups walked to- gether for a while before parting and bidding each other good night. The terrorists carried Olympic duffel bags, their weapons hidden under clothing. They encountered no guards as they made their way through the village, although six German postal work- ers had noticed the Palestinians as they jumped over the fence. To their sober eyes the men seemed suspicious. They reported the break-in, but no action was taken. Walking quickly, Issa led his men straight to 31 Connollystrasse. Arriving at the building, each one pulled an AK-47 out of his gym bag, snapped a thirty-bullet magazine into place, and slipped a round into the chamber.

7 CAPTURED

Shmuel Lalkin had always been a light sleeper. At 0415 hours he awoke in his bedroom on the second floor of Apartment 5 at 31 Connollystrasse, to the jolting sound of gunfire. He went to his front-facing window and looked out. Everything appeared quiet and peaceful in the early morning light. A chilly wind beckoned him back to bed. "Maybe a nervous sharpshooter unintentionally discharged a round," he thought to himself. The exhaustion of the past few days weighed on his eyelids. He planned to wake up in less than two hours.

A few minutes earlier, the terrorists had reached the blue door leading to Apartment 1. It was open, as always, since it led not only to the Israeli dorms but also to the parking garage and the upstairs housing units. The terrorists walked through a small foyer to the door of Apartment 1, home to seven Israeli coaches and referees. The terrorists had a copy of the key. One of them slipped it into the door; the lock wouldn't turn. The jiggling of the key woke Yossef Gutfreund, a six-foot-three, 285-pound international wrestling referee. Gutfreund, forty, married, and the father of two young girls, had refereed at the 1968 Mexico City Olympics. Though he was a businessman by profession, the Romanian-born referee devoted much of his time to sports. He rolled out of bed and made his way toward the jarring noise.

The terrorists flipped the lock and opened the door. Gutfreund stood in the hall, barefoot, in his underwear, peering at the armed and masked men facing him. He immediately recognized the men's intentions: Arab terrorists are coming to take us hostage. "Guys, run!" he shouted at his six sleeping roommates. Gutfreund threw the full weight of his body against the door. The terrorists, who realized they'd lost the element of surprise, pushed with all their strength. Gutfreund was an overpoweringly strong man, but the terrorists managed to wedge the steel barrel of a Kalashnikov between the door and the frame and use it as a crowbar. The former wrestler, knowing he could not hold them for long, struggled selflessly, buying time for his friends to come to their senses and escape. The only way out was through the back window.

The weight lifting trainer, Tuvia Skolsky, a Holocaust survivor who had lost his entire family on German soil, heard the sounds of Gutfreund's desperate struggle. He bolted out of bed and into the living room, where he saw Gutfreund grappling with the half-open door. On the other side he clearly saw a man in a black ski mask prying the door open with his weapon. "I understood that I needed to escape immediately," Skolsky, the only survivor from Apartment 1, said in his testimony. He yelled to his sleeping flatmates to run for their lives as he raced to the back window.

Everything happened quickly. Only ten seconds had passed from the moment Gutfreund blocked the door until Skolsky reached the window. The lock stuck. Skolsky knew his life was in immediate danger. Flustered and panicked, he punched through the thick double glass, cutting himself on the remaining shards as he threw himself out the window. He jumped to his feet and ran.

By now the terrorists had overpowered Gutfreund. They charged into the room and began shooting at Skolsky through the broken window. "I could hear the bullets whistling past my ears," he reported. He ran through the courtyard garden, barefoot, in his pajamas. He slipped behind the corner of the building and crouched down, stunned.

The gunfire that almost killed Skolsky was the same gunfire that roused Lalkin.

Back in Apartment 1, the terrorists herded the six hostages into a second-floor bedroom and began binding them with the precut rope they had brought with them. They marched Gutfreund to the corner of Apartment 1, keeping a weapon trained on his face. They yanked the other five from their beds: Amitzur Shapira, a forty-year-old track and field coach and father of four; Kehat Shorr, fifty-three, the marksmen's coach; Andrei Spitzer, twenty-seven, the newly married fencing coach and father of a one-month-old daughter; Yaakov Springer, fifty, a weight lifting referee officiating at his fifth Olympic Games; and Moshe "Moni" Weinberg, thirty-three, the wrestling coach and father of a newborn son. Unlike the rest of them, Weinberg was not drowsy. He had just sneaked back into the apartment after a night out with friends in Munich. A strong man, used to close-quarter battle, Weinberg lunged at Issa, knocking him off his feet. But before he could grab his weapon, a second terrorist, acting instinctively, shot a single round that ripped through his right cheek. Blood poured from his mouth, staining his clothes and the floor beneath his feet. The terrorists pushed the hostages into Shorr and Spitzer's room on the second floor. They were all bound at the wrists and ankles.

The men sat stunned on the two simple beds, most of them in their underwear. Issa and two of the masked men remained with the hostages, guns pointed at their heads. Tony, the second in command, and the four other terrorists took Weinberg with them and set out to find more Israelis. Outside they passed by Apartment 2, housing five Israeli track and field athletes, and charged into Apartment 3. Weinberg, bleeding, was forced to lead the terrorists through the apartment complex to the Israeli rooms, an AK-47 at his back. Despite everything, he kept his head clear. Apartment 3 housed the wrestlers and the weight lifters. Weinberg, their coach, must have reasoned that the big boys had the best chance of overpowering the terrorists.

Tony and his men surprised the athletes who shared the two floors of Apartment 3: David Berger, twenty-eight, American-born weight lifter; Eliezer Halfin, twenty-four, lightweight, Soviet-born wrestler; Mark Slavin, eighteen, Greco-Roman wrestler, also from the former Soviet Union and the youngest member of the Israeli delegation; Yossef Romano, thirty-two, middleweight, Libyan-born weight lifter, and father of three girls; Ze'ev Friedman, twenty-eight, a featherweight, Polish-born weight lifter; and Gad Tsabari, a light flyweight freestyle wrestler. The terrorists quickly pulled the athletes out of bed. Shouting and butting them with their weapons they corralled the Olympians in the living room on the first floor. While three of the terrorists kept the athletes under watch, one of them looked under beds and in closets for hiding Israelis. David Berger, who held a law degree from Columbia University, turned to his friends and whispered, in Hebrew, "Let's charge them, we've got nothing to lose." One of the terrorists caught the whisper and immediately slammed the barrel of his weapon into Berger's back, shutting him up and stymieing, for the time being, any chance of a revolt.

Yelling and jabbing, the terrorists forced the athletes into a straight line with hands clasped on their heads. They marched them outside, back in the direction of Apartment 1. Wrestler Gad Tsabari, weighing less than 106 pounds, was first in line. As they walked through the blue door into the foyer of Apartment 1, one of the terrorists, a ski mask covering his face, directed Tsabari into the apartment with a jerk of his gun. "I was dazed and sweaty," Tsabari recalled. "Without thinking too much I slapped aside the barrel of his weapon and ran outside." He took the winding stairs down to the underground parking garage in giant leaps. One of the terrorists followed him down the stairs and fired a few quick shots in his direction. But Tsabari, who zigzagged and took cover behind the pillars of the building, remained unscathed.

Moshe Weinberg, the wrestling coach, stood farther down the line. He held a piece of cloth to his injured cheek as they marched outside the apartment complex. While Tsabari was running through the underground garage, Weinberg took advantage of the momentary distraction and made a move for one of the terrorist's guns. His sudden movement alerted one of the other terrorists, who released a long burst of fire, stopping Weinberg in his tracks and ripping his chest apart. The remaining hostages were shoved into Apartment 1 without further incident. Less than ten minutes had elapsed.

The village woke up to the long, thumping burst of gunfire that killed Weinberg. Lights went on in rooms, heads poked out of windows. Lalkin jumped out of bed. The major now knew this was not accidental fire. Nothing could have prepared him for what he saw beneath his window. On the sidewalk, outside Apartment 1, Weinberg lay lifeless, his clothes soaked in blood.

Lalkin looked to his right and saw Henry Hershkowitz, the flag bearer at the opening ceremony, gaping out the window of Apartment 2. The two of them watched an Oly make his way toward the building, walkie-talkie in hand. Minutes before, a call from a cleaning woman had alerted the authorities to the sound of gunfire. At 0450 hours the security shift manager sent a guard to check the scene. The guard saw Weinberg's body splayed on the ground and one of the terrorists near the blue door. He turned to the armed terrorist for an explanation, but got no response. The unarmed Oly radioed back to headquarters, describing what he had seen.

Lalkin raced to the first-floor living room, to the only phone in all of the Israeli housing units. He knew part of his delegation had been seized and that at least one member was dead. He got an outside line and called the Sheraton Hotel, where all the Israeli journalists and Olympic officials were staying. "Call Israel!" he said. "Arab terrorists have taken part of our delegation hostage."

Again, he looked out the window: several unarmed guards had congregated outside Apartment 1. He patted his hip, where the firearm he had been refused might have been resting. He thought for a moment how much safer he would feel if he had a gun. He rechecked the lock on the door and went back to the phone, maintaining his connection with the outside world. Remembering his son's pleas to stay with the wrestlers in Apartment 3 brought a wave of nausea. He chased the thought from his mind.

Meanwhile, in the room where the hostages were being held, wrestler Yossef Romano, who had torn tendons in his knee and was using crutches, began to contemplate a desperate move. He had witnessed Weinberg's attempt to seize a weapon, had seen him killed; nevertheless, he lunged at one of the terrorists, grabbing for his gun. He managed to put the terrorist flat on his back but was shot by another one of the hostage takers. Romano's dead body was left in the center of the living room. Nine hostages remained.

The phone rang in Manfred Schreiber's apartment shortly after 0500 hours. Schreiber, a solidly built man in his late forties, was the all-powerful chief of the Munich police, responsible for planning and running security at the Olympic Games. He immediately ordered the village guards to isolate the Israeli dorms and lock the gates to the village, preventing anyone from entering or leaving. He placed one call, to Bruno Merck, before leaving his house. Merck, the interior minister of Bavaria, contacted Hans-Dietrich Genscher, the German interior minister. Within an hour, all of West Germany's top officials had been updated. They were stunned, embarrassed, and, primarily, uncertain how to proceed.

Police were sent to the home of Olympic Village mayor Walter Troeger to wake him and escort him to the scene. The smooth politico was completely unprepared for what awaited him. Just after 5:30 A.M. the authorities scooped Moshe Weinberg's lifeless body off the sidewalk outside Apartment 1 and placed it in an ambulance. On September 5, 1972, the people of Munich awoke to the sound of sirens and the rumble of dozens of military trucks. Flickering police lights painted the city blue at dawn.

The international media began issuing reports, mostly of an uncertain hostage situation in the Israeli housing units and one confirmed dead body that had been cast out into the street. In America, ABC held the exclusive television rights to the 1972 Munich Olympic Games. Their morning coverage began with sports reporter Jim McKay saying, "The Olympics of Serenity have become the one thing the Germans didn't want it to be: the Olympics of Terror."

Hundreds of reporters rushed to the scene, gathering bits of information and rumor. At first, Israeli journalists reported that sixteen to seventeen hostages had been taken. Later, the number was reduced to thirteen. Only when Tsabari and Skolsky together with the athletes in Apartment 2 were located could journalists report, with a degree of certainty, that there were ten Israeli hostages. Many hours would pass before the terrorists would reveal the second dead hostage. Even then, they refused to divulge the man's identity or allow his body to be removed.

The terrorists released two pages of tight typewriter script, containing the names of the 236 prisoners whose release they demanded, 234 of whom were held in Israeli jails. Among them were Kozo Okamoto, the Japanese terrorist who had attacked passengers at Lod Airport, and the two Palestinian women who had carried out the Sabena hijacking. The additional two prisoners, the notorious urban guerrillas Ulrike Meinhof and Andreas Baader of the left-wing Red Army Faction, were held in West German jails. The terrorists demanded that all the prisoners be released by 9:00 A.M. and transported to an Arab country. Only after that would the Israeli hostages be freed. If their demands were not met, they would execute a hostage every hour.

Signed: BLACK SEPTEMBER.

8 BUNGLED NEGOTIATIONS

The 0900 deadline was impossible to meet. The West German and Bavarian officials gathered in the basement of the G-1 administration building in the Olympic Village were ill equipped to deal with a hostage situation. They had neither the time nor the know-how to craft an effective plan. The only task they addressed was forestalling the deadline. A Bavarian policewoman named Analiese Graes, who had volunteered to serve as an intermediary between Issa, the German-speaking terrorist leader, and the German officials, arranged a meeting outside Apartment 1.

At 0845 hours, Manfred Schreiber, the Munich police chief; Walter Troeger, the mayor of the Olympic Village; and Ahmed Damardash Touni, the Egyptian delegate to the International Olympic Committee, made their way up Connollystrasse to meet with Issa. A terrorist with a ski mask over his face and a Kalashnikov in his hand stood by the second-floor window and watched the German officials approach. Issa, in a cream-colored suit and an oversized white hat, immediately stepped out of the building to greet them. It was to be the first of many meetings.

Schreiber was impressed by Issa's composure and his fluent German. "He expressed his demands succinctly, forcefully, calmly, and tirelessly," he later said. Issa never showed his eyes. He was polite and, at times, friendly with the German officials, but behind his dark sunglasses, the wiry, chain-smoking terrorist clearly controlled the situation. He clutched a grenade in his hand at all times, ready to release the pin and kill them all at the first sign of trickery.

Troeger and Schreiber had no protocols to work from and no clue how to neutralize the situation. Touni, a native Arabic speaker, was asked to negotiate with Issa in the comfort of his mother tongue. He assured Issa that German and Israeli officials in Bonn and Jerusalem were looking into his demands, but they needed more time to process "the details." Issa immediately extended the deadline till noon.

Schreiber, a veteran police officer used to dealing with an array of criminals, considered grabbing Issa and using him as a bargaining chip. Issa caught his roaming eyes. Lifting the grenade, he said, "If you lay your hand on me, I'll blow us both to bits." A move like the one Schreiber considered might have worked against a group of criminals committed to cash rather than a cause. But the Palestinians in Apartment 1 were devoted to an idea, not to one another. They would never have negotiated for Issa's life. After all, it was he, in the train station, who had told them they were all martyrs for the Palestinian cause. And with him gone, they would have become more volatile, unpredictable, and difficult to deal with.

Throughout the hostage crisis the negotiating team showed their ignorance of the goals of ideological terrorists. Schreiber offered Issa "an unlimited amount of money" in exchange for the Israeli hostages. He suggested they set the sum. "This is not about money," Issa replied with disgust. "Talk of money is demeaning."

Hans-Dietrich Genscher, the portly, jowly West German interior minister, also failed to grasp the essence of the terrorists' mission. "When it became clear to me that the negotiations were off course I said to the leader: 'You know our history, you know what the Third Reich did to the Jews. . . . You need to understand that that can't happen in Germany again.' I told him to take me instead of them." Genscher's pleas fell on deaf ears.

At 1045 hours, Genscher, Merck, and Schreiber established an official crisis committee. The Federal Republic of Germany had no hostage negotiation team, and the men seemed lost, adrift, lacking in ideas, yet unwilling to accept advice. Ulrich Wagner, an eyewitness to the hostage crisis and an aide-de-camp to Genscher, later said, diplomatically, "At this time, we were, I think, a little bit naïve." Weeks after the crisis, the federal government chose Wagner to establish and command the GSG-9 anti-terror unit—an outright result of that naïveté.

Black September stood firm; for them there was no way back. The terrorists were willing to become *shuhada,* martyrs; in fact, it was an integral part of their plan. Troeger, who spoke with Issa at length, relayed his sentiment: "Either way we are dead. Either we will be killed here, or if we go out and give up without having hostages . . . we will be killed where we go."

Troeger likened Issa and his men to the Japanese kamikazes of World War II. In the early 1970s, words like "martyr" were rarely heard in Europe and America. Suicidal terrorists weren't commonplace. But the death-by-martyrdom notion was well entrenched in the Arab Muslim culture to which the terrorists belonged. Despite the fact that the armed Palestinian resistance was, at the time, secular and, to a large degree, under the spell of Marxist ideology, the Black September terrorists were devotedly suicidal.

The West German, Bavarian, and Olympic authorities had one goal: to remove this stain from their event as soon as possible and resume the Games. But as noon approached, the West German negotiating team was no closer to a solution than they had been six hours before. The Palestinian terrorists would not bend: they wanted prisoners released before they would begin to discuss freeing the hostages. The Israelis, led by Prime Minister Golda Meir, refused to bow to extortion. The negotiations, as an end in themselves, were futile.

The Germans also had to address Israel's demands that the Games be halted until the end of the crisis. The West German authorities refused. The main events would go on. And so, as nine Israeli athletes sat in their Olympic dorm, hands and feet bound, thirsty, hungry, frightened, and sweaty, their friend's body in a pool of his own dark blood, a host of assault rifles in their faces, three thousand fans gathered to watch Japan's skilled volleyball team drub West Germany.

Neither the Olympic organizers nor the German officials thought this strange. Eventually, once Israeli pressure turned international, the IOC and the German authorities agreed to halt the Games briefly at 1530 hours and to hold a memorial ceremony for the two fallen athletes at ten the following morning. They had no way of knowing that the memorial would take place as planned, but for many more than two.

9 GOLDA BLANCHES

Victor Cohen called his wife and asked her to pack him an overnight bag. Cohen, head of interrogations at the Shabak, had spun a web of hope around the Sabena hijackers four months before. Minutes earlier Yosef Harmelin, the widely respected head of Shabak, had called him. "Get to Lod Airport immediately," Harmelin said. Cohen understood—he was to fly to Munich to negotiate with the terrorists who had taken the Israeli athletes hostage earlier that morning.

When Cohen, a stout man with quick eyes, walked into the packed, smoked-filled airport VIP room, he saw Defense Minister Dayan, Mossad chief Zvi Zamir, and his boss, Harmelin, conversing in a corner. He was taken aside and told that the prime minister had decided to send Dayan and Zamir to Germany. Dayan, he was told, insisted that Cohen accompany them.

At 0530 hours Prime Minister Golda Meir had been awakened with news of the attack in Munich. At first, her military aide,

Brigadier General Yisrael Lior, was unable to sketch a clear picture of the events, but by nine, when an emergency meeting of the defense cabinet was set to begin, certain facts had been established: Moshe Weinberg, the wrestling coach, had been killed; nine or ten Israeli athletes were being held at gunpoint in their apartment complex in the Olympic Village; Fatah's Black September group was responsible; the terrorists demanded that Israel release over two hundred prisoners.

At the close of the meeting Meir and her cabinet decided that the Israeli ambassador to West Germany, Eliashiv Ben-Horin, would present the following principles to the West German authorities:

1. The Israeli government does not bargain with terrorists. The responsibility of handling the crisis falls on West Germany. The Israeli government expects the West German government to do all in its power to secure the release of the hostages.
2. Israel will understand if the terrorists are promised freedom, so long as it helps liberate the hostages.
3. Israel hereby pledges its trust in West Germany and is certain that the government will do all in its power to ensure the safety of all the hostages.

Ben-Horin arrived at the Olympic Village at 1100 hours under direct orders from Jerusalem. He was the first official Israeli representative to meet with the negotiating team. He immediately relayed the cabinet's position, emphasizing Israel's absolute refusal to release terrorists from its jails. Ben-Horin kept the diplomatic channels open for both formal and informal messages.

The talks with West Germany were burdened by the stress of the present and the oppressive weight of the past. Since early morning, Meir, German chancellor Willy Brandt, and Interior Minister Genscher had held a drawn-out and unproductive dialogue over the phone. Chancellor Brandt and Genscher voiced their disgust at the attack and expressed condolences over the death of Weinberg. They had little else to offer. Meir, for her part, clarified her position—that the West German government was responsible. Brandt and Genscher did not dispute that, or ask for greater flexibility on the part of the "Old Lady" regarding the terrorists' demands. They did, however, politely refuse the prime minister's offer to send a team of commandos to Munich.

Brandt's and Genscher's hands were tied by German federal law. Israeli officials were unaware that the German constitution did not give the federal government authority to move so much as one soldier into the Bavarian state. Constitutionally, all matters concerning the resolution of the developing international crisis were in the hands of the Bavarians, sole sovereigns of the Olympic Village. Brandt's and Genscher's degree of influence was tied to the Bavarians' willingness to heed their advice. However, any intervention, foreign or federal, was deeply resented by the Bavarian authorities.

The German reputation for precision, efficiency, and order inspired confidence in the Israeli leaders. Dayan and Zamir were certain that the West German security forces would stage a well-designed rescue. They didn't realize that the Federal Republic of Germany lacked an anti-terror unit, and that, even had such a unit existed, it would not have been able to act in Munich. No one in Israel thought to check these facts.

At 1450 hours Golda Meir stood before Israel's parliament, the Knesset, in a two-piece Terylene suit, her gray-streaked hair pulled back in a bun, and announced that Israel "expects that the Federal Republic of Germany and the International Olympic Committee will do all in their power to free the Israeli citizens from the hands of the murderers. It is unfeasible that the Olympic Games will continue as though nothing has happened while our citizens are under the threat of death at the Olympic Village."

Prime Minister Meir and the top officials of Israel's security forces concluded the emergency meeting by deciding to leave the rescue mission in German hands. In an interview fifteen years after the massacre, Zamir said, "There was a bad feeling about whether the Germans could really be trusted. Could we remain uninvolved when questions of what, how, and why arose?"

Moshe Dayan, who held enormous sway with the prime minister, pushed for Israeli abstention from the hostage crisis. Other officials urged Dayan to fly to Munich, as head of the defense establishment and the Israeli with the greatest influence abroad.

Victor Cohen arrived at the airport ten minutes after Dayan. Cohen disagreed with the decision to send Dayan. He approached the legendary general, who was talking with Zamir and Harmelin, and said, "Listen, the hostage situation is playing out in front of the world. If you show up there, the media will recognize you, the terrorists will hear about your arrival, and then they'll understand how major this crisis is for Israel, and that doesn't help us at all. It will only make them raise their price and maybe rattle them enough to harm more hostages. You should stay in Israel."

The room fell silent as all heads turned to Cohen. Dayan's decisions were not often questioned in public. Dayan nodded. "You're right, Victor. You and Zamir should go. I'll notify Golda."

A few hours later Cohen and Zamir boarded a rented plane for the three-and-a-half-hour flight to Munich. They touched down at Munich International Airport as the last flicker of twilight played on the plane's metallic wings. A secret service car took them straight to the Olympic Village.

Concurrently, Golda Meir spoke to a reporter in her office. Why wasn't Israel willing to bargain with the terrorists? the reporter asked. "If we should give in," she replied, "then no Israeli anywhere in the world will feel that his life is safe." After a few beats of introspection, she added, "It's blackmail of the worst kind."

10 IN THE HOSTAGES' ROOM

Issa agreed to extend the deadline three times. First, under pressure from Schreiber, Troeger, and Touni, he gave them one hour. Merck and Genscher were then able to squeeze two more delays of two hours each, making the new deadline at 1700 hours. The Germans explained that the postponements were merely bureaucratic: the Israelis had not yet been able to locate all 234 prisoners; there were difficulties obtaining the approval of one minister; Tel Aviv traffic is stifling. Their excuses, some plausible, some less so, were meant to give the impression that negotiations were progressing, strings were being pulled, prison doors were sliding open on well-oiled tracks. The end of the crisis was near—a bit more patience and the terrorists would be parading through the joy-filled streets of Beirut, held aloft by a throng of supporters.

With each delay, Issa became more impatient and volatile. When the third extension was requested he threatened to execute two of the Israeli hostages. He vowed to drag the athletes to the doorway and shoot them in front of the cameras. Across the globe a billion viewers were glued to their televisions, watching the crisis unfold in real time. Tension peaked in the minutes leading up to each of Issa's deadlines. In those nerve-racking moments, the German negotiation team would walk to the entrance of 31 Connollystrasse. Issa would huddle with the group. The viewers could see but not hear. The conversation over, the Germans would move slowly away from the building. The world held its breath waiting for the TV announcer to broadcast the verdict from the West German officials. With the approach of each deadline the athletes' families watched helplessly as the delegation's fate was discussed.

As the crisis on Connollystrasse boiled and simmered, athletes in the village soaked up the sun. Two hundred yards from the Israeli delegation's building, sunbathers lay on the banks of an artificial pond. The Olympians chatted about the competition and exchanged training techniques, while just two minutes away their fellow competitors were being held at gunpoint, their lives in peril.

The scene at the village was surreal. The Munich police estimated that seventy thousand spectators, alongside thousands of reporters, television crews, and photographers with long-range lenses, tried to get close to the action. Athletes and troops shared the same ground, the former chatting and staying loose, wary of taking their minds off the prize of Olympic competition; the Olys, police, and soldiers stood by armored personnel carriers, focused on the looming possibility of a gunfight.

At 1635 hours, close to twelve hours of static negotiations ended when the gloomy German officials presented themselves at the blue door. Their strategy was leading to a dead end, and they knew it. The Bavarian interior minister, Bruno Merck, spoke first, but with little success. The terrorists weren't buying any more half-baked excuses. Issa then surprised the Germans with a new proposal. He demanded that a plane be ready and waiting on the runway within an hour. The terrorists and their hostages would be flown to Cairo, where the negotiations could continue. The Israeli government would fly the released prisoners to Egypt, and the exchange would be made there. If this demand was not met, Issa assured them calmly, he would execute each and every one of the hostages.

Genscher, Schreiber, Troeger, and Merck backed away from the doorway to confer. They agreed that the plan was not viable. The sovereign nation of West Germany could not allow the transfer to foreign soil—the kidnapping, actually—of international guests by a terrorist group. Yet Issa's proposal also held considerable appeal. The shift of the crisis to an Arab country might save the Olympic Games: with the crisis two thousand miles away and far from the prying lenses of the media, the so-called Games of Peace and Joy could go on.

The crisis committee wanted to buy time to see if the plan was in any way workable. Genscher asked to speak to the hostages. Issa hesitated for a minute and then shouted to Tony in Arabic on the second floor. The curtains at the second-floor window were opened and fencing coach Andrei Spitzer appeared in his undershirt. His hands were tied, his hair plastered to his sweaty forehead. "Is everybody okay?" Genscher asked. "What is the situation with all the other hostages?"

Spitzer managed to reply, "Everybody is okay except for one—" before he was hit in the back of his head with the butt of an AK-47 and dragged away from the window. This implausible encounter, captured by the cameras, was the last time Spitzer was publicly seen alive.

Genscher insisted that Issa let him into the hostage room. He wanted to see the athletes with his own eyes. If they were willing to fly to Cairo, West Germany would arrange the transfer. Issa was feeling the pressure: he and his squad had been on their feet for at least twenty-four hours. They had been holding the hostages captive for twelve. He knew their lack of sleep could compromise the mission; he feared losing the ability to make sharp decisions. The negotiations were going in circles. Egypt had friendly relations with Fatah; they would be welcomed there. Issa understood that the longer they stayed in the Olympic Village, the more vulnerable they became. He assumed that the Germans were just waiting for the right moment to pounce. The move to an Arab country, which first came up as a possibility during the planning stages of the operation, now seemed a brilliant option. And if Cairo should reject the planes, they would simply fly on to Morocco.

Issa also recognized that one battle had already been won—that of the airwaves. Throughout the hostage crises the Palestinian problem had been prime-time news; millions of people now knew of their people's predicament. Issa agreed to Genscher's request.

At 1705 hours, five minutes after the final deadline passed, Genscher and Troeger pushed open the blue door, entered Apartment 1, and bounded up the steps to the room holding the captives. The view was harsh. Weight lifter Yossef Romano lay lifeless in the center of the room, in a spreading pool of blood. The walls were stained red and riddled with bullets. Food and garbage was strewn across the floor. Yossef Gutfreund, the hulking weight lifting referee, was bound to a chair. The remaining eight hostages were crammed together on two beds with their hands and feet tied. "It was a terrible impression," Troeger later recounted. "Appalling, I must say. They said they were treated well; however, the discussion was absolutely overshadowed by the fearful and depressed mood of the hostages." Genscher, who was shaken by the encounter, said, "The picture of the room will stay with me as long as I live. I will never forget those faces, full with fear, and yet full of hope."

Genscher introduced himself to the hostages as the interior minister of West Germany. He spoke softly in German and Troeger translated. Genscher promised the Israeli hostages that he would do everything possible to help them. "How do you feel?" he asked. He glanced at the face of each man in the room and then asked whether they were willing to be flown abroad with their captors. The hostages nodded numbly in agreement. Genscher and Troeger filed out of the room. Troeger once again requested that he be held hostage in place of the Israeli athletes. Again, Issa refused.

The German incompetence during the hostage crisis was absolute. Their feeble attempts to free the Israelis were pathetic, doomed to failure. Schreiber was the first to propose "kidnapping" Issa, during their first, early morning meeting. After that, the negotiations team suggested snatching several of the captors as they came out of the apartment to pick up four heavy crates of food. Two undercover policemen wearing chefs' uniforms complete with toques planned to help carry the food, then spring into action and overpower the terrorists. The scheme was inane. Issa requested that the food be delivered at 1400 hours, then brought in each crate by himself. To prove that the food was not poisoned or drugged, German tasters sampled each plate.

The next scheme to free the Israelis was equally harebrained. After lunch, twelve local policemen, chosen for their martial arts skills, were stationed on the roof of 31 Connollystrasse. Their orders were to burst into Apartment 1 through the air-conditioning vents and the windows. Their codeword: Sunshine. Ulrich Wagner, who would later become an expert in hostage negotiations, felt that the rescue team was unfit for the job. "They selected them, asking: have you shot a gun or whatever? That was it; they had no training, nothing."

After going over the layout and position of the building's air vents, the policemen were instructed to take over the roof. The inexperienced volunteers wore training suits over bulky bullet-proof vests. Their mission: to surprise the terrorists and extricate the hostages without causing them injury.

Codeword Sunshine was never spoken. Live TV coverage showed the rescue team standing on the roof in their training suits. Every room in the Olympic Village had a TV: Issa watched the events unfold, in real time, on his own personal screen. He stepped out of the apartment yelling at the Germans that two hostages would be killed immediately if the police did not get off the roof. At 1800 hours, Schreiber gave orders to retreat, and the amateurish rescue mission was aborted.

Schreiber and his men tried to get an exact count of the number of terrorists they faced. Knowing their number would be essential to any successful rescue mission. They identified four terrorists, including Issa, simply because these men had popped their heads out of the second-floor windows and the third-floor balcony. The four-man count was revised once Genscher and Troeger returned to the crisis center and reported that there were at least four or five terrorists in the apartment. Miscounting your target guarantees failure. Schreiber and his men thought they were facing five terrorists—which is partly why, four hours later, their rescue mission would fail so abysmally.

II   DESTINATION: CAIRO

The German plan was simple. The terrorists and their nine hostages would be transferred to Fürstenfeldbruck military airfield, where two separate police units would be waiting in complementary ambushes. The first would be sprung on the terrorist commanders. The Bavarian officials assumed that Issa and his deputy, Tony, would inspect the plane and the crew that would fly them to Cairo. Thirteen officers of the police special task command force, dressed as stewards and cabin crew of the Lufthansa Boeing 727, would ambush the terrorists as soon as they boarded.

A second squad of five sharpshooters would act once Issa and Tony were caught inside the plane, neutralizing the terrorists and liberating the hostages. Armored personnel carriers would then swoop in and pick up the weary Israeli athletes. Georg Wolf, police chief Manfred Schreiber's deputy, was selected to command the rescue operation. The men at his disposal were novices, entirely lacking experience in counterterrorist maneuvers.

• • •

Zvi Zamir and Victor Cohen arrived in Munich as Troeger, Schreiber, and Merck were discussing the final details of the Cairo transfer with Issa. They met with Ambassador Eliashiv Ben-Horin, who introduced them to Genscher and Franz Joseph Strauss, a senior Bavarian politician. Genscher and Strauss took the Israeli officials to meet Schreiber and Merck. The Bavarian officials were outspoken in their opposition to Israeli interference in the hostage crisis. "My presence bothered them," Zamir later recalled. "My very arrival bothered them. It was so bad that they actually tried to bar us from the Olympic Village and were unwilling to speak with us."

Complex internal German politics were putting the hostages at even greater risk. Zamir, an introvert with an inexpressive face and tight lips, was bounced from one German administrator to the next. He began to comprehend the complexity of the relations between the West German government agents and the Bavarian officials. "During the rescue [the federal agents] didn't say a word," Zamir recalled. "They didn't intervene, even once. They sat where they were told to sit and they stood where they were told to stand."

Initially, Schreiber and Merck refused even to discuss the details of the rescue mission with the Israeli representatives. "I remember, to this day, the police commander's answer," Zamir said. "It still rings in my ears. He said, 'This is what we want: to get them to the airport. There everything is prepared for the release of the athletes.' As I understood it, they already had a comprehensive plan." Though Schreiber's and Merck's cold and aloof attitude did not make a favorable personal impression, Zamir felt a great sense of relief when they at last announced they had a plan. "I thought: a miracle is happening. There is a plan, preparations are being made. There are snipers. West Germany's reputation preceded them, this was not a developing country. We were encouraged."

In the evening hours, fervent plans were being discussed at 31 Connollystrasse. One final hitch remained: how would the captors and the hostages be transported to Fürstenfeldbruck airfield? Issa wanted a bus to deliver them. Schreiber and Merck insisted they fly by helicopter. Despite their differences, the Bavarian and West German officials had come to agree on one basic principle: the captors could not be allowed to leave the country with the hostages. As Troeger explained in a later interview, "We tried to give the terrorists the impression that we'd let them fly out but then tried everything to kill them or capture them before they could leave the country."

Shortly after 1830 hours, Issa, who began to see traps behind every twist in the plan, agreed to travel by helicopter to the airport. He had been told that the Olympic Village was surrounded by thousands of angry protesters who were blocking the roads, and that he and his men would probably be overwhelmed and lynched if he attempted to make the twelve-mile journey to the airport by bus. Genscher told Issa the helicopters could be readied in two hours. Departure from the Olympic Village was scheduled for 2100 hours. Issa's behavior made it clear that his deadline's elasticity had been stretched to the fullest.

A wave of uncertainty was rising over the hundreds of radio and television crews broadcasting from the Olympic Village. The German press officials were slow to release new information, and when they did, it was often one bit at a time. Rumors circulated in the press pool. Around the world viewers hunkered in front of their TVs, watching and waiting for the outcome.

Genscher, Merck, Schreiber, and Troeger arrived at the blue door at 2050 hours. They told Issa they had organized a four-man volunteer aircrew to fly the helicopters to Fürstenfeldbruck airfield, where a Cairo-bound plane was waiting on the runway. The German team asked Issa for his word that the flight crew would not be taken hostage or harmed in any way. Issa promised to respect their neutrality. The officials then explained that the terrorists and their hostages would have to walk two hundred yards to the helicopter landing pad. Issa agreed, but first insisted on inspecting the route. He told his men to kill the Israelis if he did not return within six minutes. His accomplices nodded, all too aware that the Germans might be on the verge of springing a trap.

Issa left Apartment 1 with Schreiber, Troeger, and several police commanders. They walked down the stairs to the underground parking lot at 31 Connollystrasse, on their way to the improvised landing pad behind administration building G-1. A second Palestinian gunman walked behind the group, his weapon aimed at their backs.

As soon as he entered the parking lot, Issa saw shadows darting between the concrete pillars. He vetoed the two-hundred-yard walk. They would be too exposed on the way to the landing pad. The group returned to Apartment 1. The shadows in the darkness, police gunmen, had missed their opportunity. Issa now demanded that a bus take them to the waiting helicopters.

The Germans searched for an appropriate bus. They found a willing driver and a minibus with sixteen seats. Issa took one look and refused to board. He wanted a full-sized bus. Schreiber's men searched the Olympic Village till they found a driver willing to take the captors and hostages to the landing pad. Slightly after 2200 hours the bus's engine was humming in the underground parking lot of 31 Connollystrasse. At 2205, the first terrorist went down the stairs and opened the door leading to the garage, AK-47 in hand. He combed the area with his eyes, looking for anything out of the ordinary. Satisfied, he signaled to the others. The terrorists pushed the hostages out of the building in groups of three. The Israelis were blindfolded and bound to each other at the waist, their hands tied in front of them, as they were shoved onto the bus. The tension was escalating. The terrorists, suspicious of even the slightest movement, waved their weapons in the air, stabbing at the threatening darkness that surrounded them.

The bus rolled slowly toward the landing pad, taking several minutes to make the two-hundred-yard journey. Two Bell helicopters were waiting, their flight crews in place. Inspecting them with a high-powered flashlight, Issa was first off the bus. He checked the two aircraft for anything out of the ordinary and then signaled the other terrorists. Four hostages were taken off the bus: Berger, Friedman, Halfin, and Springer. They were loaded onto the back bench of the first helicopter. Tony, the second in command, rode with this group, along with three of his men. Issa, in charge of the second helicopter, boarded with the three remaining terrorists and the five other hostages.

Shmuel Lalkin, head of the Israeli delegation, stood on the balcony of the administration building, watching as the hostages were herded into the helicopters. "The helplessness left us with a grave feeling," he later said in anguish. The Israelis were completely vulnerable, like lambs to the slaughter.

Zamir and Cohen stood next to Lalkin. "There was a deathly silence," Zamir recalled. "It was a terrible scene. We had a hard time watching it: we were standing on German ground, watching shackled Jews being taken to helicopters."

The night was illuminated by thousands of camera flashes. The remaining Israeli athletes huddled together on the balcony, watching in disbelief. "This isn't a goddamn James Bond movie," muttered one, as he watched the media frenzy beneath him. "This is life and death."

Zamir and Cohen stood next to Bavarian prime minister Franz Joseph Strauss and German interior minister Hans-Dietrich Genscher. "Suddenly I heard Strauss say to Genscher in German, 'Hey, they got the number of terrorists wrong!' " Zamir later recalled. "I was struck by his words. I realized that they hadn't known up until that point how many terrorists there were, despite the fact that they had been inside and spoken with them. Suddenly, as they're walking to the helicopters they realize they got the number wrong. It hurt. I noticed that Strauss was shocked too. It was a serious blow to the German devotion to accuracy. I was sure that they had stationed five sharpshooters on each terrorist. They gave me the feeling that the plan was tailor-made, that they had thought of everything, and then . . ."

12 THE CATASTROPHE

GERMANY, FÜRSTENFELDBRUCK AIRFIELD
TUESDAY, SEPTEMBER 5, 1972, 2200H

The two helicopters rose off the pad and slipped into the darkness. As soon as they were out of sight, a third chopper arrived. Senior federal and Bavarian officials ran out of the administration building and down to the landing pad. The Israeli envoys, Zamir and Cohen, were once again surprised to find themselves persona non grata. Bavarian officials tried to block them from stepping up into the waiting helicopter. "It's full," they said. Zamir and Cohen pushed past them and sat down, glowering.

They flew directly to the Fürstenfeldbruck airfield, while the choppers, carrying the hostages and their captors, flew a preplanned, circuitous route. The German and Israeli officials landed ten minutes before the other helicopters and headed straight for cover in an administration building at the center of the airfield, next to the control tower.

Ten minutes later, at 2236 hours, the two helicopters carrying the eight terrorists and the nine hostages touched down. Issa jumped out and hurried toward the Lufthansa Boeing 727 waiting a hundred yards east of the control tower. Tony jumped out of the other helicopter and ran after Issa. Four terrorists, two from each helicopter, stood guard outside their respective aircraft. The German pilots left the controls and stood stiffly beside the choppers, at attention, as though waiting for a superior officer.

Issa had no way of knowing of the drama that, moments before, had taken place on board the cold Boeing 727. Twenty minutes earlier a group of thirteen officers from the police special task command force had abandoned the plane—and their mission—for "fear for their lives." The senior German officials hiding out in the office building next to the control tower were equally ignorant of these critical developments.

The policemen, under the command of Reinhold Reich, had aborted their mission while the helicopters were in the air, fifteen minutes before the terrorists and hostages landed at Fürstenfeldbruck. Reich, a rookie in all matters concerning counterterrorism, had, unbelievably, put the mission to a vote. The decision to abort was unanimous.

Later Reich shamelessly explained that their decision hinged on operational instructions that seemed suicidal. Their commanders, Schreiber and Wolf, supported them wholeheartedly.

It is possible to understand some of Reich's claims and still reject their validity. At the heart of the matter lay negligence and a glaring lack of professionalism. Wolf and Schreiber were negligent because the plane in which their planned ambush was to take place was carrying 8,300 liters of high-octane, highly flammable fuel. A hand grenade, or even a bullet, could have engulfed the police crew, the nearby helicopters, and the hostages in a massive fireball. If the authorities had already decided that the plane would not take off, why not empty its tank of fuel? Reich was also correct to note that his men would hardly have passed as airline flight attendants: many wore Lufthansa shirts but police-issue trousers. Uniforms that fit the flight crew could easily have been found. It is also reasonable to understand Reich and his men's contention that the mission leaned toward the suicidal. But the timing of their decision to abort—while the helicopters were in the air—remains manifestly unacceptable. It was their duty to point out these faults early in the afternoon, during the planning stage of the mission. Had this been done, the risks could have been diminished to a level he and his men could accept.

Issa and Tony boarded the plane. It was cold, dark, and empty. The aircraft did not seem travel-ready, though, as the West German officials had promised it would be. The two terrorists quickly reversed course, moving back toward the helicopters in front of the office building. The tension built in the second-floor room where Zamir, Cohen, and the German officials sat in darkness. They peered out the window.

Someone whispered, "What's happening?"

The Bavarian group recited the main points of the plan, adding sheepishly, "We don't exactly know what's happening."

At the same time, Georg Wolf, the commander of the rescue effort, was lying on the roof of the building. He already knew that the special task command force had abandoned their mission, but had yet to be informed by his superior, Schreiber, that his five marksmen were preparing to act against eight—not five—heavily armed terrorists. Only four minutes had passed since the helicopters had landed. Six of the eight terrorists were in the sights of the marksmen. Two of them, Issa and Tony, the leaders, were in motion. At 2240 hours, Wolf ordered Marksmen 4 and 5, who were lying next to him, to open fire.

Their fire was trained on two of the four terrorists guarding the helicopters. Only one was hit and neutralized. The others scrambled under the helicopters and returned long bursts of automatic fire in the direction of the tower and the lights. The first two shots were a signal to the other marksmen to open fire.

Marksman 3 dropped Tony on the tarmac with a shot to his foot. Issa zigzagged his way, firing quick bursts of 7.62mm rounds at the control tower and the office building as he ran toward the cover of the helicopters. For several long minutes the terrorists unleashed wild automatic fire and threw grenades at the tower. They hit most of the lighting giraffes, throwing the landing pad into darkness. It was now impossible to differentiate between terrorist and hostage. Drama was becoming tragedy.

Sporadic exchanges of fire pierced the darkness. The number of terrorists injured or dead was unknown. Jamal Al-Jishey's finger was crushed by a bullet, his weapon mangled. A German policeman was shot through the head by a stray round. Fifteen minutes into the mission, all that could be reported was chaos. The German officials on the second floor had no idea what was happening, and couldn't pull themselves together. Schreiber admitted as much in his later testimony: "We all felt paralyzed. The only person who exploded in rage against the perpetrators was the former Minister-President Strauss. He screamed at them and cursed them. The rest of us were incapable of doing even that."

Sporadic fire was followed by twenty minutes of tension-filled silence. Zamir and Cohen were shocked by the turn of events. Realizing that help would not come from the command center, they decided to take the initiative, find a police official, and have him issue an order to storm the terrorists. The official refused, telling them that he had decided to wait for the armored police vehicles. When they arrived, he explained, their forces would approach under the cover of armor. Once again, negligence was the order of the day. The armored vehicles should have been ordered to leave the Olympic Village hours before, but that order was never issued. Ten minutes into the firefight, the armored vehicles were finally told to move. They were then stuck in a massive traffic jam, unable to maneuver around the numerous cars of curious bystanders who had flocked to the scene of the hostage crisis.

Zamir, in a desperate, final attempt to convince the police officer to fight, pointed to two German air force pilots lying, seemingly injured, on the asphalt next to the helicopters. The police officer remained resolute: he would wait for the armor.

The silence stretched. The marksmen were unable to locate the terrorists in the dark shadows beneath the helicopters. The terrorists, it seemed, were saving their ammunition. Zamir and Cohen climbed on the roof to get a commanding view of the scene below. They saw two German marksmen, holding their fire, unable to discern friend from foe. Cohen lifted a megaphone and spoke in Arabic to the terrorists: "Give up. Save yourselves." Their answer came in a hail of bullets.

In the officials' room, Ulrich Wagner, standing next to Interior Minister Genscher, turned to one of the senior police officers with a desperate plea. "What are you going to do? Pull out the hostages! Do something!"

The commander, lowering his eyes, said, "I have no orders."

The situation had reached a stalemate. It was almost midnight. An hour and twenty minutes had passed since the chaos commenced. Suddenly, four armored police vehicles lumbered out of the darkness. The terrorists felt the immediate shift in the balance of power. The end was coming. They were on the brink of failure and the hostages were still alive. One of the terrorists leaped out of the helicopter under Tony's command and threw a fragmentation grenade inside. The grenade exploded, setting the fuel tanks on fire. A sky-licking flame rose up, illuminating the tarmac. The fate of the shackled hostages within—Ze'ev Friedman, Eliezer Halfin, David Berger, and Yaakov Springer—was sealed.

Seconds later, another terrorist jumped into the second helicopter, where Yossef Gutfreund, Kehat Shorr, Mark Slavin, Amitzur Shapira, and Andrei Spitzer sat, hands and feet manacled, bound to each other. He must have seen their terrified faces as he sprayed them with automatic fire from close range. Wagner heard their final cries above the rattling gunfire.

In the moment of silent shock following the massacre, the remaining terrorists jumped to their feet and started to run. They fired at the control tower as they fled into the darkness of the surrounding fields. One of the marksmen was able to catch Issa in his sights and kill him. Three of the terrorists, Adnan Al-Jishey, the injured Jamal Al-Jishey, and Mohammed Safady, made it to the open fields along the runway. The German police chased them in armored vehicles, on foot, and with dogs for over an hour before they were caught.

One helicopter continued to burn, yet no one extinguished the fire. The firemen on hand were unwilling to approach the scene, deterred by the occasional gunfire. They waited until all the terrorists had been caught before putting out the flames with foam. David Berger's life was lost as a result. The bodies of the three athletes sitting beside him in the helicopter were destroyed by the fire, but Berger's remained intact. He had been shot, perhaps by both police and terrorists, in the calf and thigh—nonfatal wounds. David Berger, an autopsy revealed, died from smoke inhalation.

13 IT'S ALL OVER

"I hope I'll be proven wrong but that last explosion—the one after the shooting—didn't sound good to me. I hope the German broadcaster was right. I don't have a good feeling about this. I won't say the Israelis are safe and sound until I see them with my own eyes. I hope to be back on the air in the morning with more encouraging updates and reports of a positive outcome. Good night." This was how Yeshayahu Ben-Porat, a leading Israeli radio reporter, closed a virtual marathon of live coverage from Munich.

Several minutes later, Zamir and Cohen stumbled out of the administration building, through the smoke and smoldering ash, to the two deathly still helicopters on the tarmac, hoping to find survivors. "I descended the stairs," Cohen recalled, "and went over to the first helicopter. There were spreading pools of blood around and under the helicopters. The doors were open and I saw a horrifying vision of five hostages, tied together and stuffed into the back bench, each man's head resting on the shoulder of the man next to them. There was no movement, not a groan or a raspy breath, and the blood, the blood was flowing out of the helicopter and collecting in puddles on the asphalt. I saw no need to go over to the second helicopter, the burnt one. We were shocked. Total silence surrounded us. Genscher and Strauss came out of the office building and walked over to us. They shook our hands, and mumbled some words of consolation."

The helicopters had taken off for Fürstenfeldbruck at 2200 hours, leaving hundreds of journalists behind, while hundreds of millions of viewers across the world remained riveted to their screens, waiting to see how the saga would play out.

Once the helicopters left the Olympic Village, reporters were starved for credible information. Precious time elapsed until they learned that the terrorists and their hostages had flown to Fürstenfeldbruck airfield (and not Munich International Airport). Reporters were forced to serve up live, on-air speculation about every rumor that floated their way. It was impossible to cut the live broadcast and promise a roundup later in the night. The news stations' prerogative held sway: the show must go on.

Thousands of reporters and spectators gathered behind Fürstenfeldbruck's outer fences. They had been denied entry, and in the darkness, hundreds of yards away, it was difficult to discern what was happening on the airfield. A general assumption spread through the crowd: the terrorists would be transferred from Fürstenfeldbruck to a Middle Eastern country, with or without the hostages.

This optimistic assumption was dashed at the sound of gunfire. As the firefight continued, uncertainty and confusion grew. Technical problems prevented radio and telephone communication between the officials stationed at the airfield and the administrators at the Olympic Village.

Rumors raged. Slightly after 2300 hours, a report circulated among the spectators at the airport gates and spread to the Olympic Village: the Israeli hostages had been rescued following a battle between the police and the terrorists; the terrorists had all been killed. In the absence of any real knowledge, this ideal outcome was exactly what people desperately wanted to believe, and it was presented as fact. The source of the information was unclear and yet everyone—reporters, politicians, bystanders, and family members—clung to it. Reuters, the international news agency, sent out an exclusive wire report at 2331: "All Israeli hostages have been freed."

All attempts to check the facts with officials at Fürstenfeldbruck failed. Despite the lack of confirmation, the pressure on German chancellor Willy Brandt to go on the air and announce the good news to the German nation was immense. His political instincts would not allow him to do it, however. He sent his press secretary, Conrad Ahlers, to speak to ABC's Jim McKay around midnight. "I am very glad that as far as we can see now, this police action was successful. Of course, it is unfortunate that there was an interruption of the Olympic Games but if all comes out as we hope it will . . . I think it will be forgotten after a few weeks."

The good news spread like wildfire through the Olympic Village and around the world. At last, a happy ending. The village erupted with celebrating athletes popping champagne corks, hugging, smiling, and crying with joy. The members of the International Olympic Committee along with German and Israeli politicians relaxed for the first time in nineteen hours. In Israel, relatives and friends showed up at athletes' family homes with flowers and champagne. For most Israelis it was difficult to hold their spontaneous joy in check. They did not heed Yeshayahu Ben-Porat's advice to wait until the hostages appeared before the cameras.

For the families of the hostages, caution came by instinct. Ankie Spitzer, the wife of fencing coach Andrei Spitzer, was at her parents' home in Amsterdam. A wave of joy swept the room when they learned of the Reuters news flash. People jumped to their feet. Ankie, composed, told everybody to wait. "Andrei will call and when we hear his voice, we'll celebrate," she told her family. A similar scene played out at the Gutfreund and Springer homes. Rachel Gutfreund, wife of the towering wrestling referee, refused to celebrate even when her children joined in the general revelry. Rosa Springer asked that her guests not open the champagne until she heard her husband's voice.

Ankie, Rosa, and Rachel would never hear those voices. The truth reached the media just after three in the morning. At 0317 hours Reuters sent a corrected message over the wires: "Flash! All Israeli hostages seized by Arab guerrillas killed."

Jim McKay immediately broadcast the devastating update to the world. He looked straight into the camera and said: "I have just gotten the final word. When I was a kid my father used to say, 'Our greatest hopes and our worst fears are seldom realized.' Tonight, they have been realized. . . . They've now said that there were eleven hostages. Two were killed in their rooms yesterday morning. Nine were killed at the airport tonight. . . . They are all gone. It's all over. . . . I have nothing else to say."

Half an hour before the world heard the news, just before three in the morning, the head of the Mossad, Zvi Zamir, placed a call to Prime Minister Golda Meir's private residence in Jerusalem. It was the first thing he did upon returning to the Olympic Village. He had not heard the false reports of safety or the celebrations they had sparked. The prime minister grabbed the phone on the first ring. Zamir spoke first. "Golda . . . I have bad news," he said softly. "We just returned from the airport, all nine were killed . . . not one was saved."

Golda could not believe it. She had been watching TV and listening to the radio.

"But they reported . . ." she protested, trying to stave off the dreadful truth, shocked and dejected.

"I saw it with my own eyes," Zamir said. "No one was left alive."

More than two thousand journalists from all over the world gathered at daybreak at the Olympic Village's communications center to listen to West German and Bavarian officials recount their version of events. They carefully avoided taking any personal or state-level responsibility for the tragedy. Instead they blamed the Israelis and the Palestinians: the Israelis were faulted for their intractable refusal to release Palestinian prisoners; the Palestinians, they claimed, performed their deadly mission with such accuracy and skill that the Germans were powerless to prevent the tragedy. "Some people say that police mistakes caused the death of the hostages," Manfred Schreiber, the Munich police chief, said. "But it was the other way around. The hostages died because the terrorists made no mistakes."

• • •

The German failure has no modern equivalent. The amateurishness, negligence, miscalculations, and mistakes made in the management of the crisis are unparalleled. To this day, no one has ever claimed responsibility for the failure to stop the Olympic massacre: not the Bavarian government, not the Federal Republic of Germany, nor any other German office.

The errors in the planning and organization of the police rescue mission at the Fürstenfeldbruck airfield under the command of Georg Wolf, as supervised by Schreiber, are particularly intolerable and maddening. They do not comprise the Germans' only failures but are worth examining. The operational components of the plan attest, at best, to the unprofessional and negligent handling of the mission. At worst, the results of the mission point to a reprehensible cowardice and an unforgivable dereliction of duty. The squad in the field had five hours to prepare for the mission, which is an eon in a hostage situation. The mission was ideally staged—in a military airport, with no civilians nearby. The police could easily plan where the helicopters would land and at which angle they would be placed in relation to the marksmen. They could have blinded the terrorists with carefully positioned lights and orchestrated a well-timed strike.

The colossal failure of the marksmen is particularly inexcusable. From the internal West German report completed after the operation, it came to light that the five marksmen, two of whom were Bavarian riot police and the other three Munich policemen, were chosen based on a competition held months earlier. They had never received professional training as sharpshooters. They had no special abilities as far as psychological condition, shooting techniques, and operational tactics were concerned. "I had no special training in gun shooting or anything similar. But I practiced pistol shooting as a private hobby," Marksman 2 said in his debriefing.

These so-called marksmen were given G3 and FN rifles, which are far from tactical-level precision weapons. They were on duty from the early morning. At 2240 hours, some of them had been on their feet for fourteen to fifteen hours, which robbed them of the inner calm necessary to function as a sharpshooter in the tense, potentially chaotic storm of a hostage liberation mission.

Another element of the negligence and amateurishness of the operation was rooted in the lighting setup. Three Polymar reflectors, known as lighting giraffes, were brought to the scene on Wolf's orders. There was no moon, and the reflectors were not strong enough to light up the night. An ideal lighting situation would either have blinded the terrorists and left the sharpshooters in the dark, like the audience in a theater, or kept the scene in total darkness and equipped the sharpshooters with infrared scopes, which would have afforded them a tactical edge over the terrorists. The pale middle ground created a situation where the marksmen could not tell whether the terrorists in the shadows beneath the helicopters were alive or dead, and left the inside of the helicopters, where the hostages sat shackled and terrified, as dark as a cavernous hole at night.

The police gunmen were unprotected. They had no helmets and no bulletproof vests. But the worst sin of all was in the communication between forces. In order for a sniper strike to have any hope of success, the attack must begin when each shooter has the head of his prey square in his sights. A commander then commences a slow countdown, allowing each sniper time to communicate last-second changes. As the countdown nears the "fire" command, each sniper steadies his breathing, so that they pounce together, squeezing the trigger in unison, as they exhale the last of a calculated breath. In that way the element of surprise is preserved, each terrorist taking a bullet at the same time. The importance of a communication system is vital to the success of a counterterrorism mission, which is often complex and continuously shifting. In this instance, a proper communication system would have enabled the authorities to pass on the actual number of targets in real time.

An enduring question from that day revolves around the number of marksmen. The police had nineteen gunmen available that day. In any special operations mission, there should be at least two skilled snipers per target. In this situation, where the men lacked experience, visibility was poor, and targets were mobile, they should have stationed three or four, even five shooters on each terrorist. Schreiber explained that he needed to keep some of his men in reserve in the Olympic Village and some of them at Munich International Airport in case the terrorists decided to change course. Still, the answer does not satisfy the question of why the central arena of operation, the Fürstenfeldbruck airfield, had less than a third of the available Bavarian marksmen.

• • •

For years after the massacre, victims' family members sought information that would shed light on the circumstances of their loved ones' deaths. There were many unanswered questions. They sought access to autopsy logs and ballistic reports. "I wanted a full account of what really happened from the Germans," Ankie Spitzer said. "Nobody seemed to be able to explain who was at fault. Who shot whom at the airport?"

The German government instituted a red-tape jungle of bureaucracy, shuffling requests from one office to another without providing any answers. After several years, the Germans claimed that they did not have any evidence from the crime scene. This made Ankie Spitzer suspicious: it did not seem possible that such a ghastly and public tragedy would go uninvestigated. A proud and graceful woman who speaks Dutch, German, English, French, and Hebrew fluently, Spitzer refused to accept Germany's excuses. She demanded to know what really happened in Munich on every commemoration day, in each public forum, in the pages of all the newspapers.

For more than thirty years, Ankie Spitzer and Ilana Romano, widow of Yossef Romano, have been representing the interests of the bereaved families. The two women have met with almost every high-ranking German official who has visited Israel since 1972. In these brief meetings, grudgingly agreed to by the Germans, Spitzer and Romano requested the release of all the documents pertaining to the Munich Massacre. For over two decades promises were made and then broken by the German politicians. The reports never arrived.

The German authorities hoped that the Israeli families' resolve would weaken, but the two widows did not relent. Sparks of hope were lit and then left to flicker. The Germans did not intend to release any information on the subject. They certainly were not going to accept any responsibility or apologize for the massacre on their soil.

The greatest disappointment came in 1976, when Hans-Dietrich Genscher, the interior minister of Germany at the time of the massacre, came to Israel on an official visit as Germany's foreign minister. Genscher had remarked that the day he walked into the hostages' room in Apartment 1, saw the dead man splayed on the floor, the blood in a puddle by his feet, and the terrified look on the hostages' faces, was the worst of his life. Yet he refused to meet the representatives of the families. Only Ankie Spitzer's desperate threat to prevent his plane from taking off convinced his assistant to schedule a meeting with Spitzer and Ilana Romano at the West German embassy in Tel Aviv. Their meeting began at six in the morning and lasted fifteen minutes.

Genscher sat silently through Spitzer and Romano's presentation. They requested that all previously withheld information about the event be released. They asked that West German authorities draft a compensation plan for the surviving families, and build a memorial for the victims. Genscher listened stone-faced. He said he would reply to their requests in writing. His answer arrived at the Foreign Ministry in Jerusalem ten months later.

The official letter was so inadequate, it was disrespectful. Genscher denied government possession of documents relating to the Munich Massacre. As for compensation, Genscher wrote that the West German government was prepared to grant scholarships to two of the children of the victims for one year of study in West Germany. The scholarships, according to Genscher, would only be given to children who could prove financial need. The letter did not address Spitzer and Romano's request for a memorial. The compensation plan did not even attempt to meet the needs of the thirty-four widows, fatherless children, and bereaved parents whose lives were devastated by the massacre. The families refused to accept the inadequate offer, and resolved to continue their fight for information.

Spitzer and Romano did not receive a significantly greater degree of assistance from the Israeli government. Though the eleven murdered athletes and coaches had been sent to Munich to represent the state, Israel offered neither political nor financial help to the families. Left alone to deal with the implacable German federal authorities, Spitzer and Romano were forced to manage an international dialogue from their homes, rather than through proper diplomatic channels. There is no clear explanation for Israel's official policy—their unwillingness to pursue the truth of that night.

A conflict of interest may explain their reluctance. In the 1970s, security ties between Israel and West Germany were greatly expanded, and West German intelligence agencies worked closely with their Israeli peers. Joint secret missions and intelligence exchanges were carried out on a regular basis. Sayeret Matkal and the Yamam, Israel's two leading counterterror units, assisted the West German government in establishing the German GSG-9 counterterror unit, under the command of General Ulrich Wagner.

Twenty years of deadlock came to an end in the spring of 1992. Several weeks before the twentieth anniversary of the massacre, Ankie Spitzer made an emotional appeal to German viewers in an interview on ZDF television. She spoke of her fruitless quest to discover the truth about the Munich Massacre and her husband's death. She reiterated her refusal to accept German claims that there were no documents from that night. Spitzer stole viewers' hearts with her powerful message, delivered in German.

Two weeks later, she received a call from an unidentified German government official. "There is information, you're absolutely right," he said. "I have access to the information." Spitzer had been plagued for years by crank callers pushing conspiracy theories and false information. She dismissed the man as another such and directed him to Pinchas Zeltzer, the Israeli lawyer representing the victims' families. Zeltzer, however, took the caller seriously. The German government worker told the lawyer he had access to documents. He offered to send a sample of the papers. "I've been waiting for this material for twenty years," Zeltzer told him. "Send everything you can." Zeltzer promised to keep his source confidential, come what may.

A messenger arrived at Zeltzer's office door two weeks later holding a brown envelope with original documents from the West German investigation of the massacre. There were thirty pages of autopsy logs for Andrei Spitzer, David Berger, and Yossef Gutfreund. There were ballistic reports on almost all the eleven victims. In total, there were eighty original typewritten pages collected from different dockets, suggesting a wealth of documents amassed by the German authorities in the aftermath of the massacre. They had been stored in the Bavarian archives for twenty years, hidden from the eyes of the public.

Ankie Spitzer was elated. After two decades of battling the German authorities, she finally had access to the truth. She was closer than ever to being able to reconstruct the final hours of her husband's life.

Once the authenticity of the documents had been verified, Spitzer demanded that the federal government provide her with full access to the archive. The government refused. After several TV appearances, a political storm erupted in Germany. During one dramatic debate, Spitzer, speaking live from Tel Aviv, confronted the Bavarian justice minister, who denied the existence of any official archives; Spitzer produced a sheaf of papers and began quoting from the official ballistic reports.

The German opposition party demanded the release of the information. The interior minister of Germany and the Bavarian justice minister were in the hot seat, trying to cover up two decades of dishonesty.

On August 29, 1992, Zeltzer received notice from Munich: "We found the documents. You can come to Munich with a local lawyer and collect everything we have."

The next day Zeltzer flew to the Bavarian capital to scour the municipal archives. In the basement of the archives building, twenty boxes and crates stuffed with dusty files were presented to him. There were 3,808 files holding tens of thousands of documents. There were hundreds of investigative reports, dozens of eyewitness accounts from everyone who had participated in the rescue mission, and nine hundred invaluable photographs, mostly taken after the massacre. It was an incredible collection of material, carefully detailing the events of September 5, 1972, allowing the families to finally learn the truth about how their loved ones had died.

The material also enabled the families to file a legal claim for compensation. In 1972, when the struggle with the German authorities began, there were thirty-four parents, widows, and children involved. By the time the case was brought to court in the mid-1990s, only twenty-five remained alive. The case against the federal government, the Bavarian government, and the municipality of Munich was brought to court in 1994. After years of exhausting legal negotiations in the Bavarian court system, a deal was offered to the families. "If you continue in the courts we will no longer speak with you," top officials in Berlin said to Ankie Spitzer in 2003. The Germans offered a settlement of 3 million euros, to be divided among the twenty-five complainants, which came to $115,000 per person.

The families held a tempestuous meeting in Tel Aviv in 2004. Two alternatives were presented. The first: accept the financial offer and forgo the opportunity of forcing the German federal government, the Bavarian state government, and the Munich municipal government to be held accountable for their actions. The second: refuse the offer and continue the indefinite legal battle for at least eight more years.

After long deliberations, the families decided to accept the German offer. Only Ankie Spitzer wanted to keep fighting. "I was disappointed by the decision but I understood the circumstances which led to the vote going the way it did. It wasn't money that mattered. The lawsuit for monetary compensation, from my point of view, was the only way to force the Germans to deal with and to reveal what had happened, to take responsibility and to announce their guilt and even, maybe, to request to be forgiven. After more than thirty years, we managed to make them bend. Even if they didn't directly state their guilt, they understood that they were responsible."

15 TOUGH DECISIONS

The "Voice of Israel," the country's public radio station, began its top-of-the-hour news broadcast with a series of high-pitched, solemn tones. The headlines followed. On Thursday, September 7, at ten in the morning, the lead news item detailed the burial times for ten of the victims of the massacre.

An El Al Boeing 707 carrying ten coffins was due to land at Lod Airport at 1145 hours. Israel had withdrawn from the Games and the surviving Israeli athletes and delegation members were on board as well, accompanying their slain colleagues. Funerals would take place immediately following a brief military ceremony at the airport. The eleventh victim, weight lifter David Berger, had been flown from Germany earlier that day. President Richard Nixon had sent an American air force plane to bring the athlete's body back to his hometown of Shaker Heights, Ohio.

The Israeli government declared September 7 an official day of mourning. The nation was traumatized. Flags were lowered to half-mast; stores, restaurants, and government offices were closed. People clustered in the streets, reading the papers in groups, learning the anatomy of the tragedy.

The Munich attack was unlike anything the young country had weathered. It was a dividing line, separating history into "before Munich" and "after Munich." Israel had known trying hours before, but Munich cut through all its defensive layers of scar tissue and sinew. Jews had been led yet again to their death on German soil. Images of the athletes, Israel's finest, bound, unable to resist their impending death, tore deeply into the nation's psyche. A feeling of helplessness prevailed. Only twenty-seven years had passed since six million Jews had been herded into camps and murdered. Now, the wounds of the Holocaust bled again.

The Mossad department responsible for gathering operational intelligence on terrorist organizations was humming with frenetic activity. An emergency draft had quadrupled their workforce overnight. New recruits, who had passed the rigorous entrance exams two months earlier but had yet to begin the case officers course, were called in to assist the department's five permanent staffers.

The Mossad staff officers crammed into three small rooms. Their task was to review every personnel file, to reread every piece of data, to find threads and expose connections that would lead them to the identities of the planners and perpetrators of the Munich Massacre. They needed to understand and unmask Black September, and identify its links to Fatah and the PLO.

Over the ensuing weeks and months they would sift through tens of thousands of raw intelligence reports. Mossad personnel stayed up late and worked weekends. Emotions ran high; commitment was total: everyone knew the significance of the quest.

Failure, frustration, and shock were written across Zvi Zamir's face that morning as he made his way to his tenth-floor office. Three floors below, at the Tzomet (Crossroads) wing of the Mossad, the feeling was equally dour. Tzomet case officers (*katsas*), operating from Europe, drafted and ran Arab agents that were either part of, or subsequently inserted into, the military, political, and economic spheres of all Arab countries. This human intelligence—HUMINT—was, in the 1970s, Israel's primary means of discovering the intentions and capabilities of its enemies. But the focus had been on Syria and Egypt—Israel's neighbors to the north and south—where the threat of war loomed. Terrorist organizations were a bit neglected.

Nonetheless, for the past forty-eight hours Tzomet staff officers had been grappling with a frustrating and demanding question: How did we not sound the bell? How did we not learn of the plan? How did we so utterly fail to pick up a single bit of intelligence about this attack, which must have required a considerable time to plan, and certainly included a few dozen people? One day earlier, just twenty-four hours after the hostage situation came to its tragic end, Zamir had commissioned an internal investigative team to examine the Mossad intelligence failure. It was already clear that no one in the Israeli intelligence community had so much as one quality HUMINT source in Black September or the group surrounding Abu-Iyad or Ali Hassan Salameh at the upper echelons of Fatah.

* * *

All Palestinian terrorist organizations raised their level of alertness. They were poised for the scripted retaliatory air strikes that generally followed a major attack. This time, even the Syrian and Lebanese armed forces began preparing for bombardment. Radio communication signals from Palestinian bases called for a mass exodus of operatives.

The wait lasted just over forty-eight hours. At 1550 hours, on Friday, September 8, on the eve of the Jewish New Year, two dozen fighter jets from the Ramat David base in northern Israel struck deep in Lebanese and Syrian territory. It was the IDF's most devastating attack in two years—air force planes bombed eleven Palestinian bases, including one just five miles from Damascus, killing two hundred terrorists and eleven Lebanese civilians. Hundreds more, both terrorist and civilian, were injured. But the dead and injured had no connection with Black September or the massacre in Munich.

At a press conference that day, IDF Chief of Staff David Elazar was asked whether the air strikes were an Israeli response to Munich.

"No," he said. "Can there be a response to what happened in Munich?"

The strikes, he continued, "were part of the war we are forced to wage against the terrorists so long as they continue to kill Israelis." When asked whether Black September had been hit, he said: "Black September is part of Fatah. We don't concern ourselves with whether or not the members of this wing are present in Syria or Lebanon. There are terrorist organizations operating from there and they have declared war on us. We must strike back."

Coverage of the Israeli strikes in the daily papers was adulatory. "The Air Force gave a 21-gun salute to the athletes, who were not honored with a military funeral," one columnist exclaimed.

Days later, IDF forces raided terrorist bases in south Lebanon: 1,350 infantrymen, forty-five tanks, and 133 armored personnel carriers, together with four artillery units and several fighter planes, took part in the mission—"Turmoil 4." One hundred fifty tons of bombs were dropped over a period of forty-two hours. Scores of villages and towns in south Lebanon, fast becoming home to terrorists expelled from Jordan, were searched. The IDF spokesman's office reported forty-five terrorists killed, sixteen Palestinian operatives captured, and hundreds of houses damaged or destroyed.

None of those killed or captured had any covert or operational affiliation with Black September. As destructive as these missions were, cabinet ministers and IDF brass knew it was not nearly enough to placate Israeli public opinion: the nation demanded a more significant form of retribution.

The public had no knowledge of a top secret meeting convened by the prime minister days earlier. On Wednesday, September 6, one hour after Zamir's return from Munich, Prime Minister Golda Meir summoned her cabinet members, among them Defense Minister Moshe Dayan and Deputy Prime Minister and Education, Culture and Sports Minister Yigal Allon to Jerusalem. They listened as Zamir, in dry but forceful words, recounted the horror of the murders he had just witnessed. The ministers were livid. A response was necessary. But many were frustrated: Who will we retaliate against? Who will we hit? Who are the commanding officers of the Black September group? Do they even have bases?

By the meeting's end they had decided on the air strikes and the subsequent ground assault, but all present recognized the need to go beyond the standard retaliatory script. The look of stern resolve on the Old Lady's face told them that she was prepared to take the difficult steps necessary. She wanted to set a new standard. She realized Israel could no longer afford to respond and retaliate. The Talmudic imperative to "rise and slay the one who comes to kill you" needed to be fulfilled to the letter of the law. A new Israeli response was needed, one that would imprint itself on the minds of conspirators everywhere, and be remembered by the free world.

16 GOLDA GOES FOR REVENGE

Lieutenant Colonel Jonathan Mor walked into one of Branch 4's two wooden shacks and shot a quick glance at the office's latest technological wonder: a twenty-one-inch black-and-white television. "What's on now?" he asked. Without turning from the monitor, Lieutenant Alik Rubin, a fluent Arabic speaker, said, "It's the Lebanese evening news. They're showing the Black September funerals, again. They were buried in the afternoon but they've been showing it in loops for hours. It's getting everyone all riled up."

The German government had agreed to the demands of Libyan strongman Muammar Qaddafi and released the bodies of the five dead terrorists, who were flown to Tripoli that morning aboard a private jet. Lieutenant Colonel Mor stood in the doorway watching the fuzzy screen for a few more minutes. Although Branch 4's antenna left a lot to be desired, the events could still be followed. They saw the sea of people bearing the coffins on upturned palms from Martyr's Square to the Sidi Munaydir cemetery. They listened to the eulogies. The dead terrorists were called "holy martyrs"—*shuhada*; their mission, "one of the loftiest, bravest, in the history of mankind." The crowd began chanting in Arabic, "We are all Black September." For days that chant reverberated in rallies throughout the Arab world—in Tripoli, Cairo, Beirut, Damascus, Baghdad—underscoring the difference between right and wrong, terrorism and bravery, in the eyes of the democratic West and the Islamic East.

The announcer on the Cairo-based PLO radio station, the "Voice of Palestine," was also turning his attention to the funeral procession of the five fallen *shuhada*. He reported the eight terrorists stated in their joint will, written just hours before their death, that their collective funds, totaling $500 and 37 German marks, were to be used in the service of the Palestinian revolution. The will read: "We are neither killers nor bandits. We are persecuted people who have no land and no homeland. We were willing to give up our lives from the very first moment." The murderers declared in their will that the nation's youth should not be afraid to sacrifice their lives for the greater goal. Every drop of spilled Palestinian blood will turn to oil and light the nation aflame with the fire of victory and independence, they said. The will contained no apology, regret, or remorse.

Lieutenant Colonel Mor left the room and walked through the other sections of Branch 4, where around twenty officers and enlisted men were huddled in small quarters despite the late hour, addressing the virtually Sisyphean task of intelligence gathering, searching for any shred of information relevant either to Munich or to future attacks. Everyone was aware that many were already eager to mimic the "success" of the Olympic attack.

Lieutenant Colonel Mor rubbed his hands together, satisfied. The following morning Branch 4 was set to open its new department—Overseas Terrorism, which would concentrate on collecting intelligence about terrorist organizations' plans against Jews and Israelis beyond the borders of the state. Additional office space for the new department would be assigned in a few weeks. The inauguration of the Overseas Terrorism department was a sign that Military Intelligence was rapidly learning the lessons of Munich.

Another result of the Munich attack was the arrival, days earlier, amidst much fanfare, of the new TV. Mor had personally requested it. He explained, "It was important we see and hear what was happening in the streets of Beirut and the rest of the Arab world. We needed more than a newspaper headline. What we wanted was to be exposed to a variety of voices and views. We knew their intentions but we needed to understand the hues and shades of their thought."

Yet another tool to come their way was a new computer, the first in the IDF's Military Intelligence division. Although everyone eagerly anticipated its arrival, no one at Branch 4 had any idea what to do with it. Their initial assignment would be to feed it tens of thousands of intelligence files.

Mor returned to his office and opened the top secret incoming telex file. Nothing noteworthy. Mor was still lacking operable intelligence. He had snippets of isolated information, tiny pieces of a sprawling puzzle. All he could report for certain was that a senior-ranking member of Fatah was responsible for the massacre.

"The massacre at Munich helped us understand that we would have to deal with a new subject that we had never before encountered—terror attacks against Israeli targets abroad," Lieutenant Colonel Mor later explained to me. "An attack on foreign territory gave the Palestinians a distinct advantage. They received international attention and our job to root out terrorists and prevent future attacks got that much harder. In terms of intelligence gathering, it meant starting from scratch, from the foundations. We didn't have hard, dependable facts. The massacre came as a complete shock; it knocked us off our feet and forced us to act under immense pressure."

. . .

At 1000 hours on Tuesday, September 12, a special parliamentary session opened in Jerusalem. All 120 members of Knesset, as well as scores of guests, stood for a moment of silence to commemorate the eleven victims of the Munich Olympics. Minutes before entering the Knesset's main hall, Prime Minister Golda Meir and Deputy Prime Minister Yigal Allon had ushered the grieving families into her office. She shook hands with the widows, the bereaved parents, and the fatherless children, offering the customary condolences. Golda's dark eyes gazed straight at them. "I want to share my plans with you. I've decided to pursue each and every one of them. Not one of the people involved in any way will be walking around on this earth for much longer," she said, pounding the table for emphasis. "We will chase them till the last." No one said a word. There was no applause. The families were far from congratulatory: they did not ask for, or desire, revenge.

The prime minister spoke from the podium at the front of the Knesset assembly hall. "The actions and ways of the terrorists are continually evolving. It is our duty to prepare ourselves for this type of war, more than we have been to this day—methodically, knowledgeably, decisively, and expansively; this is a dangerous and critical task," she said. The prime minister went on: "From the blood-drenched history of the Jewish nation, we learn that violence which begins with the murder of Jews, ends with the spread of violence and danger to all people, in all nations." At the end of her speech, the prime minister addressed the developing parameters of Israeli counterterrorism. "We have no choice," she said, "but to strike at terrorist organizations wherever we can reach them. That is our obligation to ourselves and to peace. We shall fulfill that obligation undauntedly." Meir would repeat these phrases on many occasions—they became part of the Israeli national security ethos. An entire generation of Mossad, Shabak, and Military Intelligence officers have been armed and motivated by her words.

The prime minister faced two demands in the ensuing discussion on the Knesset floor. The right-wing opposition, led by Menachem Begin and his Herut Party, demanded a parliamentary committee of inquiry. "The opposition does not accept your announcement today that the government should place the responsibility for investigating the security breach in Munich solely in your hands," said Begin, who five years later would be prime minister. "Any democratic parliament the world over would put together an inclusive, official committee of inquiry . . . so the entire nation can know what happened; what was done; what was overlooked; whether there was negligence and who was responsible for it. That is our duty."

Knesset member Shalom Cohen, of the far left, offered this: "It is our duty to ask these questions, and maybe one question more than the others: how could it have happened? . . . Especially when it was so clear that an Israeli delegation at an Olympic Games could be susceptible to this type of attack; when it is known that there are armed maniacs whose goal it is to harm us? It is our duty to tell the story of [the sprinter] Esther Shachmorov, whose mother didn't want her to compete in international competitions. She's famous, her mother said, and there are crazy people in this world. There are terrorists who might try and hurt her. She went to the authorities and to the Israeli Sports

Commission, where she was promised that her daughter and the other athletes would be kept safe. And then on the day she escorted her daughter to the airport, she saw there was no security at all. Yet they convinced her that everything was under control. . . . Let's say that out of deference to German sovereignty we were willing to forgo our desire to place our own armed guards on the ground, does that absolve us of the responsibility to check that the Germans put their own men in our stead? Was that ever checked? Now they come and tell us that there were lapses in security, but they should have seen that on the first or second day of competition; ten days went by and nothing was done. No one came to the German authorities and said: 'Thank you kindly, but you're not doing your job, so we will do it for you, otherwise we will withdraw our team.' "

The Knesset then took up the subject of Israel's response to the attack. There was wall-to-wall consensus. Begin demanded that Israel's war on terror switch gears. "Retaliation no longer suffices. We demand a prolonged, open-ended assault against the murderers and their bases. . . . We must stifle all of their plans and operations, and snuff out the existence of these murderous organizations. . . . We have the might of hand and mind; we must employ them. We need to run these criminals and murderers off the face of the earth, to render them fearful, no longer able to initiate violence. If we need a special unit to do this, then now is the time to build it."

As a longtime opposition leader in the Knesset, Menachem Begin had no idea that such a covert unit already existed. It was called Caesarea. Over the next few years the unit, which operated deep undercover, on neutral and enemy ground alike, would double and triple its budget and its manpower. Priorities were shifting all across the intelligence community and nowhere more so than in the Mossad, where Zamir, as its head, began to personally supervise the matter. The "Munich Revolution," as one renowned Tzomet division head referred to it, had begun.

Golda Meir looked up from behind a pile of paper at the men entering her office. Brigadier General Yisrael Lior, her military aide, was escorting Pinchas Kopel, the newly retired national chief of police, and Moshe Kashti, former director general of the Defense Ministry. The prime minister knew them both and went straight to the point. "Well, will you take the assignment?" she asked. The men nodded their acceptance. Golda, already in office for three long years, leaned back in her chair and set off on a maudlin monologue. She, who was so personally wounded by the murder of the athletes, was being attacked by virtually all the Knesset parties. " 'Did we have any intelligence? Any prior knowledge?' they ask. I tell them again and again that neither Zvi [Zamir] nor Military Intelligence had any sense of a pending attack. 'Why were they sent without a security detail?' " She stopped the lament and motioned them to their chairs. "I'm bearing the burden of all this, it's me they're crucifying, and now they're demanding an official parliamentary commission of inquiry. Why do you think they want that? So it can leak?"

Golda lit a Chesterfield. "Find out what happened over there, and why; interview whomever you want. You can have any documents you need." She looked over at Brigadier General Lior for approval. He was nodding. "If you run into any problems," she continued, "Yisrael will straighten them out, but you need to be quick about this. You have two weeks." The prime minister leaned out of her chair to receive an envelope from Lior. It was thick, and the words TOP SECRET were printed in bold across the front. She handed it to Pinchas Kopel. "Everything is in here. There are three copies of your mission statement. Give one to Mr. Avigdor Bartel and send him my regards as soon as he returns to Israel. The three of you are the official investigative team charged with assessing the security arrangements at the Munich Olympics."

The Old Lady, head of state and overseer of the Mossad and the Shabak, hoped that an internal investigative committee would block the growing wave of criticism that threatened to wash over her. Government ministers were already bickering and assigning blame for the security lapses, which, under the hot lights of public speculation, began to smell of ripening negligence. The public began to sense a twin failure: unfocused intelligence gathering, and a lack of security for the athletes. Some were even beginning to question the government's ability to manage the defense establishment during its counterterrorism campaign.

Golda needed a pressure valve, something to divert the stream of newspaper articles and radio reports away from the debate over culpability. The situation called for a great initiative, a measure both profound and severe. The retaliatory strikes, which bore the code name "Minor Offensive," were a temporary balm at best. They did not represent a fitting reprisal to Munich, and did nothing to help Israel in its war on terrorism. Golda realized that Israel's response had to be remorseless, had to unequivocally convey the message that, for those involved in terrorism against Israel or Israelis, death would, like the sword of Damocles, hang menacingly over every head.

That week Golda authorized the outline of a new plan to fight the burgeoning Palestinian terrorism. Drafted by Zamir and subsequently complemented by the new advisor to the prime minister on terrorism, Major General (ret.) Aharon Yariv, formerly of Military Intelligence, the plan addressed a number of issues. Chief among them was "prevention"—the elimination of terror operatives who harbored malevolent intentions toward Israel and Israeli citizens. Golda described the objectives succinctly from the podium of the Knesset one week later: "Wherever a plot is being woven, wherever people are planning to murder Jews and Israelis—that is where we need to strike."

A second, more complex element of the plan related to deterrence. The hope was that a withering series of assassinations would deter terrorists, those assisting them, and those contemplating joining their ranks. In addition, once the new strategy took hold, even the most hardened terrorists, Yariv and Zamir believed, would have to spend a great deal of their time and energy on personal preservation. The message to all terror operatives would be clear: the state of Israel will settle its score with all who have harmed or intend to harm its citizens. Israel had assassinated its enemies before, but now assassination would become a major tool in counterterrorism.

The initial and most obvious candidates were the Black September operatives responsible for Munich. They were to be found and watched until a plan to kill them could be formulated. They would lead the list; as new plots were uncovered, new names would be added. Each mission would come before the prime minister for approval. Although indictments and assassination plans would be frequently discussed with cabinet members, the prime minister alone would ultimately decide the fate of each person.

This is how it worked: A long, internal process would lead to an indictment. When the case was complete, the head of the Mossad, assuming the role of prosecutor, would argue for a guilty verdict and a death sentence; the prime minister, along with members of cabinet, would act as judges. In several instances in the months and years ahead cabinet members and the prime minister would suspend sentencing, demanding further incriminating evidence. These "trials" were top secret; aides were kept in the dark and official records bore no mention of them. Years later, the forum that decided the fate of these men was labeled Committee X by the international media.

Mike Harari, commander of Caesarea, was always present during the pseudo-trials. His staff officers and combatants would construct and carry out the operational plans. Sometimes, after detailing a proposed assassination mission, Zamir and Harari would be given the go-ahead to proceed with the planning of the mission, but not its execution: the bench accepted the prosecution's case, but withheld sentencing for a later date. Weeks, months, and sometimes years later the head of the Mossad would return to the prime minister with additional operational plans and again request authorization. The prime minister would authorize the plan only when certain that innocent civilians would not be harmed, and that the strategic interests of the state would not be harmed.

It is likely that the word "revenge" is not mentioned anywhere in the archives of government, Mossad, Shabak, and Military Intelligence documents. It was considered improper for a sovereign state to pursue revenge for the blood of the murdered. Yet it motivated, to varying degrees, every officer and official involved, from the prime minister on down.

Golda herself was wary of high-wire assassination plans. In fact, she hesitated before adopting the Zamir-Yariv plan for immediate and uncompromising retaliatory strikes. Shortly before his death twenty years later, Aharon Yariv spoke with BBC reporter Peter Taylor. "As a woman she was not very exhilarated by the idea, but I felt very strongly about it, very strongly indeed. In the end, I succeeded in convincing her. She relented."

In May 1972, six months before Zamir and Yariv's plan was drafted, Prime Minister Meir had given her authorization to kill Ghassan Kanafani, a member of the PFLP—the group that launched the Japanese Red Army attack at Lod Airport. He was an active political figure, a poet, and well-known author. His assassination, for which Israel never took credit, raised a lot of questions. Why kill a noncombatant, a noted writer? Moreover, the hit wasn't clean: a girl, who was posthumously presented as his niece, was killed along with Kanafani when the explosives attached to the chassis of his car detonated.

Golda was not the type of commander in chief to sift through operational details, asking piercing questions about proposed missions. One thought was always foremost in her mind: what will happen to the "boys" if they were caught on foreign soil? Now that she had agreed to a series of assassinations, she worried that a slipup in Europe would require a lot of difficult answers. Israel's prestige would be tarnished if it became clear that the Jewish state had stooped to the level of its terrorist adversaries. A sovereign state wasn't supposed to use the terrorists' tool—fear—or send hit squads to foreign lands.

Yet, in the post-Munich reality, Golda gave the Mossad more leeway than ever before.

• • •

Golda's predecessors tended not to use murder as a means to achieve political and security ends. Previous prime ministers had authorized assassinations only a few times in the young state's history, usually to prevent an impending attack. Every now and again an assassination plan was presented to them for approval. Levi Eshkol, the prime minister from 1963 to 1969, flat out refused to authorize such missions. His reasoning reflected sobriety: the tool of assassination is ineffective and may provoke terrorists to respond in kind. Killing would beget killing.

Eshkol had to bat down many enticing offers. An example, made public in this book for the first time, came in 1968, when Meir Amit, the head of the Mossad, requested an urgent meeting with the prime minister. A plan to kill Yasser Arafat, the head of Fatah, was in its final stage. There was something unusual in Arafat's fervor, his determination, and his steadfast terrorist ideology that indicated to the Mossad he would plague Israel for years to come. All that was needed to send him down the path to martyrdom was a nod from Eshkol.

The top secret plan called for an undercover Caesarea combatant to bring a booby-trapped car into Syria—a country officially at war with Israel—and blow it up outside Arafat's Damascus offices, where he both slept and conducted business. Yossi Yariv, the head of Caesarea at the time, had been working on the plan for six months. Only a handful of people knew the particulars. Under Yariv's directives a Caesarea combatant transferred a 1959 Chevy to Damascus. The car had made its way from Israel to Syria, via Europe and Lebanon, with one hundred pounds of top-quality explosives hidden beneath the backseat, molded in a hollow-pointed shape for optimal destruction. Once all the components of the plan were in place, Amit approached Eshkol for authorization.

"*Kinderlach*, why should I approve this?" Eshkol asked in Yiddish-peppered Hebrew. "It's a double-edged sword. Today we kill their leaders and tomorrow they kill ours. It goes on forever. I won't authorize it."

Officers at Mossad headquarters were devastated. All the preparations, planning, and risks were in vain. For neither the first nor the last time, an opportunity to neutralize Arafat was missed.

Before Munich, Arafat had been high on the Mossad's hit list, and although neither the Mossad nor Military Intelligence had the type of evidence admissible in court, both believed he knew of, and signed off on, the Olympic attack. By 1972, however, Arafat was becoming well known on the international circuit. Politics, more than state security, determined his fate. Over the years many secret meetings would be held at Mossad and Military Intelligence headquarters, weighing the pros and cons of keeping him alive. This time, Israel decided to leave him among the living.

• • •

As the Munich Massacre continued to echo across the globe, everyone in the Arab world spoke about its "success," despite the price paid by the *shuhada*, who had sacrificed themselves for the cause. The Europe-based Palestinian *saya'an*s made the most noise, eager to prove their undying allegiance to the homeland they had left. Keen to cash in on Black September's new popularity, these *saya'an*s spoke freely among friends about their involvement in the planning, execution, and logistical operations tied to the massacre. The buzz, some of it baseless bravado, reached the ears of Tzomet case officers, who were under immense pressure to deliver intelligence about the perpetrators of the attack. In the weeks after the massacre, dozens of Palestinian names, implicated by thin shards of intelligence at best, were passed back to Tel Aviv. There, they were almost automatically put on a secret database of possible targets.

The Mossad and the intelligence community, with the backing of the public consensus and the parliament, were stretching the meaning of the term "terrorist involvement" to the limit. Anyone vaguely connected to a terrorist organization or act was immediately placed on the top of a slippery slope; assassination waited below. Senior intelligence officials believed that "a terrorist is a terrorist is a terrorist." They felt that the times demanded that the gray area between guilt and innocence disappear. The head of the Mossad needed no encouragement from the prime minister. Everyone in the defense establishment was determined to avenge the murders at Munich.

18   SHADOW WARS

Five days after the massacre at the Olympics, the public was given a rare glimpse at the covert and dangerous world of a Mossad case officer—a *katsa*. On the eve of the Jewish New Year, September 10, 1972, *katsa* Tzadok Ofir received a phone call at his Brussels home. He was told that a young Moroccan man with information about Black September's operations in Europe wanted to meet him ASAP. Ofir knew his bosses at the Mossad Tzomet headquarters would want the meeting to happen immediately—despite the holiday and the history of the man requesting the get-together. Rabah, the young Moroccan exile, had offered his services to the Mossad in the past and been denied, but, days after the Olympic massacre, none of the Mossad's *katsa*s had the luxury of filtering intelligence information: anything that came in had to be turned over and examined. Black September knew the Mossad would be hungry for information, which is why they sent Rabah—a former revolutionary and current thief—to kill Ofir.

Ofir walked into the Café Prince on Place de Broker fifteen minutes early. He looked over the old, wood-paneled Victorian establishment in downtown Brussels and found what he was looking for: a darkened table in the corner, where he could keep his back to the wall and watch patrons come and go. He was alone and unarmed. Every few minutes he got up to see if Rabah was waiting outside. His gut was issuing dull pangs of warning.

Rabah arrived at 2000 hours sharp. His first contact with the Mossad had been from the Netherlands' Aranheim Prison, Cell 81. From there, as Prisoner 3382, a petty thief, he sent multiple letters to the Israeli embassy. Tzomet never wrote back. Rabah provided ample information about his past, but most of it made him appear untrustworthy. He either was or was not an officer in the Moroccan armed forces; he had been exiled from that country; he had affiliated himself with the Palestinian cause; and he had taken a number of combat courses with Palestinian terror organizations in the Middle East. During his years of exile in Europe, he crossed the law many times. The Mossad found him strange and unstable.

The barman watched as Ofir led Rabah to his table. The two were an odd couple. Rabah, in his olive-green jacket, baggy jeans, and five o'clock shadow, looked shabby; Ofir, in a leather jacket and turtleneck, was in his holiday clothes. As they made their way to the corner table, Ofir felt suddenly alone. He looked over his shoulder—Rabah was gone. On the floor was a faded brown knapsack. "A bomb!" Ofir thought. He moved to the sturdy bar, putting some distance between himself and the bag, seeking shelter from the imminent blast. As he had been trained to do, he tamped the turbulence out of his voice and asked the barman in fluent French whether, perhaps, he had seen his buddy. The barman pointed to the bathroom door just as Rabah was emerging.

"Where'd you go?" Ofir asked, approaching Rabah.

"I really had to piss. I couldn't wait."

Ofir's suspicions only intensified. Something is off, he thought to himself.

They went back to the table. Ofir sat down first. Rabah, lingering behind him, circled toward his seat, pulled out a Smith & Wesson .38, and unleashed a quick burst of fire. The first bullet hit Ofir in the ear; the second went in through his neck and out through his shoulder; the third caught him square in the chest; and the fourth went in through his shoulder and lodged itself in his stomach cavity. Ofir got out of his chair, took a few steps, and asked for an ambulance before collapsing. Rabah fled the café in a dead run as pandemonium broke out. Ofir's life was saved at St. Pierre Hospital in Brussels. The scenes from that day still haunt him.

In Beirut, Black September claimed responsibility for the hit in Brussels. The story generated enormous publicity. Papers all over the world carried accounts of the Israeli Mossad *katsa* shot by an Arab agent just five days after the Munich Massacre.

In less than a week, Black September had gone from near anonymity to public enemy number one in Israelis' perception. No one knew their next target. The defense establishment and the Mossad were asked for answers; they had nothing definitive. The files on Black September contained slivers of intelligence, bits of unchecked information that could not be cross-referenced, about operatives who may or may not have been affiliated with the mercurial organization.

On Tuesday, September 19, the mailroom in the Israeli embassy in London was bustling. Letters had piled up over the long Yom Kippur weekend, the Jewish Day of Atonement. No one in the mailroom noticed the four slim, identical envelopes sent from Amsterdam with handwritten addresses. Three of them remained sealed, but the fourth was delivered to Dr. Ami Shchori, forty-four, an agricultural attaché set to return to Israel in the coming weeks. He was chatting with a colleague when the envelope was delivered. "This is important," he said. "I've been waiting for it." He was expecting flower seeds from Holland. When Dr. Shchori opened the envelope he released a tiny spring, which hit a detonator smaller than an aspirin tablet, and set off the two five-inch strips of plastic explosive. Although they weighed only fifty grams, the explosives triggered a powerful blast, hitting Shchori in the abdomen and chest. He died of his wounds.

Black September was staying on the offensive. A week after the attempted assassination in Brussels they sent out sixty-four identical letter bombs from Amsterdam to Israeli diplomats in New York, Ottawa, Montreal, Paris, Vienna, Geneva, Brussels, Buenos Aires, Kinshasa, Jerusalem, and Tel Aviv. All of the standard-sized envelopes were detected and neutralized except for one—in London. The Israeli embassy in Kensington had been briefed about terror attacks, including the possibility of letter bombs. This was not a new tactic. The PFLP had employed the same approach to terrorism earlier in the year, sending fifteen letters from Austria and Yugoslavia to Israeli businessmen in Israel. All of them were detected and no harm was done. But the Black September campaign was far more professional: their letters bore fewer telltale signs and the explosive devices were more complex and harder to detect.

With no publicity or fanfare the Mossad refreshed its own campaign of mail-borne death. Mossad explosives experts created the letter bombs—a quick and easy way to hit senior Palestinian activists, without the time-consuming and dangerous effort required of face-to-face assassinations. On October 24, the Mossad's own campaign of terror began: Mustafa Awad Abu-Zeid suffered severe facial injuries when he opened a letter in Tripoli; Abu-Khalil, a PLO representative in Algeria, was badly wounded by a letter several days later; Farouk Kadumi and Ha'il Abed el-Hamid were left unscathed by a faulty bomb in Cairo; Omar Tzufan, a PLO activist and the director of the Red Crescent, lost all of his fingers from a letter bomb delivered to Stockholm; Adnan Hammad, a member of the Palestinian Students' Organization, was critically wounded in Bonn; Ahmed Awdullah, a Palestinian student in Stockholm accused of aiding and abetting terrorism, lost an arm.

Not one of the recipients had any direct ties to Black September. Most of the injured and the dead were PLO ambassadors and affiliates, unofficial diplomats. According to the defense establishment, though, they were field agents—Black September operatives who moved freely under the cloak of respectability while gathering operational intelligence for their masters in Beirut. The maiming of these people was meant to sow fear and confusion among activists in the PLO and Fatah's Black September. The Mossad's aim was to create a sense of permanent threat in the minds of Palestinian operatives and potential inductees, a violent persuasion to cease, or shy away from, all activity on the behalf of terrorists.

19 FIRST MAN DOWN

Mike Harari felt the familiar drumbeat of adrenaline in his neck. "The target has left the girlfriend's house. He's on his way to the bus stop," the commander of the surveillance team reported. Harari, forty-five, a chain-smoking Humphrey Bogart look-alike, checked his watch. He estimated that in just under an hour the two-week undercover operation would come to a close. He and about fifteen Caesarea combatants and staff officers under his command were on the verge of assassinating Wael Zu'aytir, the first individual to be brought by the Mossad before the prime minister and defense cabinet since the Munich Massacre.

A tall, thin man from a family of intellectuals and teachers, Zu'aytir, thirty-six, was a single Palestinian who had been living in Rome for the past sixteen years. He was presented to the prime minister and the defense cabinet as a man inextricably linked to Black September's terror operations in Italy. They were told that he was head of Fatah's Black September in Rome and that he had aided and abetted the attack in Munich. He was unceremoniously sentenced to death.

Harari didn't care to examine Zu'aytir's terrorist credentials. He saw himself as a contractor who, less than three weeks prior, had been given an assignment. His job was to fulfill the task, not analyze it. His team had been working undercover for over two weeks, on foot and in cars, from close and afar, watching Zu'aytir's every move. Now they followed him as he walked toward his apartment building in northern Rome on the Piazza Annibaliano. Just before 2230, he stopped at the Trieste bar near his house, made a phone call, and came back out to the chilly autumn air.

Two weeks of monitoring Zu'aytir led to a simple assassination plan. Zu'aytir, who worked as a translator at the Libyan embassy, was a soft target. He walked around in the open, unarmed. He allowed his habits to slip into routine. Harari and R., his chief intelligence officer, drew up a plan built on Zu'aytir's predictable schedule: two assassins would wait and then kill him at the entrance to his home.

Caesarea's surveillance team never questioned Zu'aytir's humble lifestyle, despite intelligence reports that he was a master terrorist. Unlike many PLO employees, he led a modest life. His bills were never paid on time; the telephone in his rather bare apartment had been disconnected. His circle of friends included members of the Italian Communist Party, poets, and writers, including the author Alberto Moravia. His girlfriend, Janet Venn Brown, was Australian. She was the last person he met that night. They enjoyed a pleasant dinner together.

Zu'aytir loved music and books. Before moving to Rome he'd studied classical Arabic literature and philosophy at the University of Baghdad. After studying in Iraq, he moved to Libya and from there to Rome, his permanent home. He was a gifted linguist who spoke impeccable French, Italian, and English. In his free time he read voraciously. He translated political articles and prose into Arabic and from Arabic to Italian. His greatest achievement was an Italian translation of the Arabic classic *One Thousand and One Nights*.

The Palestinian cause was undoubtedly dear to Zu'aytir, a native of the Palestinian city of Nablus, and he was in close contact with other Palestinian activists in Italy, going to rallies and parlor discussions together. But unlike many of those around him, he denounced terrorism and violence.

The Mossad did not buy into Zu'aytir's public persona. They maintained that he was a senior operative working undercover, a Jeykll and Hyde character who posed as a moderate Arab intellectual but was in fact a bloodthirsty terrorist, responsible for numerous attacks. They alleged that on August 16, 1972, he masterminded an attack on an El Al flight out of Leonardo da Vinci Airport in Rome. A tape recorder packed with powerful explosives blew up in the cargo hold as soon as the flight reached cruising altitude, but the blast was absorbed by the newly installed armored walls in the underbelly of the aircraft. The pilot, faced with a panel of screaming red and yellow lights, was able to put the plane down in an emergency landing six terrifying minutes later in Rome.

In early August, Zu'aytir was rounded up by Italian police, perhaps heightening Israeli suspicions. The police questioned him about an oil refinery bombing that had been claimed by Black September. He was released along with dozens of other Palestinians. In September, his brother, an illegal alien and a student, was thrown out of West Germany along with thousands of other Palestinians after the attack.

At 2230 hours, he walked into Entrance C of his apartment complex. He was wearing a lightweight gray blazer, a black trench coat, and a checkered shirt. He carried a basket of groceries—some rolls, a bottle of cheap wine, and a newspaper— that he had bought after leaving Venn Brown's house. Harari's combatants were spread out in their positions, alert and electric with tension. Surveillance gave the all-clear and reported that Zu'aytir was on his way to the house, alone. The escape car, a Fiat 125 that had been rented earlier by an undercover Caesarea combatant posing as a Canadian tourist, idled two 90-degree turns away.

The two assassins waited in the darkened anteroom. They watched Zu'aytir enter the building and make his way toward the elevator before they stepped out of the shadows and shot him twelve times with a silenced Beretta 0.22. He was hit in the chest and head, and dropped to the ground in a lifeless heap. The two assassins walked out of the building quickly, their guns inconspicuously by their side. The squad commander watched their backs as they made their way to the getaway car.

Minutes later, Mike Harari, his staff officers, and Zvi Zamir, who had come to Italy to personally oversee the mission, received word from the commander of the hit squad in the field. The signal released the tension in the air. Officers went from pensive waiting to quick action, gathering papers and packing bags. Within four hours, all the Mossad officers and combatants, from Zamir to the most junior member of the surveillance team, had left Italy by plane, train, and automobile.

Earlier that day, at four in the afternoon, the fourth plenum of the Knesset convened. As is customary, the prime minister delivered an address from the podium. Golda was well aware that the first act of retribution after Munich was under way. She kept her comments general. "This war, by definition, cannot be defensive; we must actively seek out the murderers, their bases, their missions and their plans. . . ." Golda refused to open the subject to debate, declaring, "I speak for the entire government of Israel when I say again that we have no choice but to strike at terrorist organizations wherever we can reach them. That is our obligation to ourselves and to peace. We shall fulfill that obligation undauntedly."

The investigation into the murder of Zu'aytir was never closed. Detectives picked up clues from the assassination site, including the rented getaway cars, but they all led to dead ends. There were no suspects and no arrests. A senior Roman police official was quoted in the next day's paper as saying that their working assumption was that the assassination was politically driven and carried out by a Jewish group.

As the mission to assassinate Zu'aytir unfolded, Golda decided to create a post in her office for a personal advisor on terrorism. She chose Major General Aharon Yariv, the professional and charming newly retired head of Military Intelligence. Some saw the nomination as a slap in the face to Zamir—a public display of no confidence. In fact, Golda recognized the need for someone to reorganize the intelligence community in a way that would allow a fluid campaign against the new threat of overseas terrorism. She needed someone willing to enforce cooperation and order among the different intelligence bodies, each insistent on maintaining its administrative and operational independence.

Yariv, fifty-two, with his piercing blue eyes, mild manners, unassuming personality, and inner calm, was the perfect man for the job. With time, the heads of the intelligence organizations realized that he did not pose a threat to their authority. As Prime Minister Yitzhak Rabin said at Yariv's funeral in 1994, "He was a man bereft of pretentiousness; who always spoke in question marks, never exclamation points, who always researched, asked, inquired, never banged on the table, and never saw himself as the final arbiter."

As soon as he took the reins, Yariv clarified the jurisdiction of each intelligence agency. He instituted a weekly forum in an office in the red-roofed, single-floor residence of the prime minister in Tel Aviv. Attending were the deputy director of the Mossad, Shlomo Abarbanel; director of Shabak, Yosef Harmelin; the head of Military Intelligence's Branch 4, Lieutenant Colonel Jonathan Mor; and several other select members—approximately ten in all. The meetings began with an overview of the week's attacks or attempted attacks. Lieutenant Colonel Mor presented the new warnings of possible terror attacks in Israel and abroad. After that the floor was turned over to the principals. They offered their interpretations of the intelligence and discussed the best course of action.

Yariv's personality was pivotal to the success of the weekly conferences. His reputation, experience, respect for others, and congeniality neutralized the fears many harbored about sharing information. The representatives of the Shabak, Mossad, and Branch 4 shared their most sensitive intelligence. "Everything was on the table," Lieutenant Colonel Mor said. "Those meetings provided the infrastructure for cooperation. What happened in there was unprecedented."

Over the years, Zu'aytir's guilt came to be taken as fact. A steady stream of intentional leaks from the defense establishment tied him to terror attacks against Israeli targets in Italy. Nonetheless, some remained skeptical about the intellectual's ties to terrorist operations. Years later, the truth seeped out. "As far as I remember, there was some involvement on his part in terrorist activities; not in operations but in terrorist activities: supplying, helping, let us say 'support' activities," Yariv explained in the BBC interview in 1993. He went on, trying to vindicate Israel's assassination campaign: "You must remember the situation. Activity continued on their part and the only way we thought we could stop it—because we didn't have any interest in just going around and killing people—was to kill people in leadership roles. And it worked in the end. It worked."

The candid interview hit members of the intelligence community like a bomb in a closed room. They were furious. It was the first time a senior Israeli official, the advisor to the prime minister on counterterrorism, had broken the code of silence.

Zu'aytir was not directly involved in the Munich Massacre. It also seems unlikely that he had an indirect hand in the operation as a *saya'an*. Uncorroborated and improperly cross-referenced intelligence information tied him to the support network of Black September in Rome. From there, a slippery slope led the politically active, low-level *saya'an* to the Mossad's hit list. Looking back, his assassination was a mistake. Undoubtedly, it resulted from the genuine desire to neutralize those involved in the Munich Massacre and "hot" operatives in the midst of preparing an attack. Zu'aytir was, at best, a small fish in a pond full of sharks. But in the vengeance-laced atmosphere of September and October 1972, when the head of the Mossad proclaimed that the mysterious, bohemian translator had blood on his hands, no one was in the mood to dispute it.

The Palestinians did not attribute the assassination to error. The "Voice of Palestine" from Baghdad announced Zu'aytir's death the following day. "The Palestinian National Liberation Movement has lost one of its most prominent, leading, and struggling members, a *shahid* and hero, Wael Zu'aytir, the representative of Fatah in Italy, who was assassinated by Zionist intelligence at 2245 yesterday when he was returning to his home in Rome."

This time, the conspiratorial Palestinian interpretation of current events was correct. The radio announcer continued in Arabic: "Fatah wishes to draw the attention of the world to the fact that the assassination of the hero Wael Zu'aytir is part of the Zionist terror campaign being carried out by the enemy throughout the world. Fatah stresses again that the pursuit and assassination of our fighters will only increase its determination to carry on with its struggle and revolution. It is a revolution until victory."

20 | THE GREAT CAPITULATION

Lufthansa Flight 615 from Damascus to Frankfurt took off at 0535 hours, with no passengers. The plane and its seven-person crew stopped in Beirut, where thirteen male passengers boarded the flight. Ten miles north of Cyprus, Captain Walter Claussen felt the hard muzzle of a pistol on the back of his neck. "I am the captain now," a soft voice said in Arabic-accented German. The hijacker took control of the intercom and introduced himself to the passengers as Abu-Ali. He informed them that the flight was now under his command. "Operation Munich," the mission to free the three Black September terrorists caught alive at the Fürstenfeldbruck airfield, was under way, he said. If the West German government agreed to free "the three heroes" of the Munich Massacre from their Bavarian jail cells, where they had been held for the past seven and a half weeks, and allowed them safe passage to a friendly Arab state, no one on the flight would be harmed; if not, he and the other terrorist on board would blow up the plane. He took his finger off the intercom's broadcast button and commanded Claussen to land in Cyprus. They would refuel before proceeding to Germany.

The West German government, without informing their Israeli counterparts, immediately decided to acquiesce to the terrorists' demands. The incarcerated Black September fighters were an unnecessary burden. Pragmatism demanded their release. Abu-Iyad interpreted Germany's decision in Middle Eastern terms: in his memoir, *Stateless,* he called it "cowardly."

Radio reports lured thousands of bystanders to Riem Airport, outside Munich, where hundreds of police, border troops, and armored vehicles awaited the hijacked plane. At 1100 hours, the Lufthansa Boeing flew over the airport but did not land, changing course for Zagreb, Yugoslavia. The hijackers altered their plans after the German authorities told them they needed ninety minutes to round up the three prisoners and bring them to the airport. The hijackers, they said, could land in Munich and wait. Claussen reported to air traffic control that Abu-Ali was storming around the cockpit, livid.

The hijackers never explained their sudden change of destination. They may have feared a ruse, a plan that would cripple the plane or a violent takeover mission designed to free the hostages. Now they altered their demands—the Palestinian prisoners were to be brought to Zagreb. The plane circled above the city, waiting for confirmation that the prisoners were on the ground, ready to be swapped. Hours passed and fuel dwindled—Claussen told his captors that there was enough fuel to last until 1730 hours.

German authorities sent a Condor passenger plane to Zagreb with the CEO of Lufthansa, two police officers, two replacement pilots, and the three prisoners. As the plane approached the Yugoslavian city the two sides had yet to reach an agreement about the terms of the prisoner exchange. The government proposed a simultaneous trade: the Palestinian prisoners for their citizens; Abu-Ali agreed—the three men would be brought on board and flown to an Arab state, in return for the hostages. The German decision was influenced by the pleas of the Lufthansa pilot, who warned that the plane was running perilously low on fuel. "Please hurry up," he said. "These are our last moments." When the 727 finally touched ground on the heels of the Condor, there were only two hundred liters of fuel left in its tank—enough for thirty more seconds of flight.

The three newly freed prisoners bounded up the stairs to the plane, but in violation of the agreement, the hijackers refused to free the hostages—they all took off for Libya. At 2100 hours, the Boeing 727 reached Tripoli. The hijackers and the released prisoners, who had been partying throughout the flight, were greeted like kings upon arrival. While the West German ambassador to Libya arranged for the immediate return of the hostages to Germany, the freed terrorists held a press conference. International audiences both heard the terrorists' firsthand version of events in Munich and witnessed the complete capitulation of the German government.

Chancellor Willy Brandt explained Germany's actions in his own words. "The passengers and the crew were threatened with annihilation unless we released the three Palestinian survivors of the Fürstenfeldbruck massacre. Like the Bavarian government, I then saw no alternative but to yield to this ultimatum and avoid further senseless bloodshed."

Brandt neglected to mention that West Germany felt threatened by the terrorists incarcerated on their soil. Pressure from Arab countries to release the three had been building since the massacre, and reports of possible revenge operations against Germans and Germany were pouring in. It was only a matter of time before a hijacked plane or some other extortionate measure would "force" the Germans to release the three terrorists, who were, after all, putting German lives at risk.

German, Palestinian, and Israeli sources contended that the

hijacking, carried out by PFLP specialists under the command of Wadi Haddad, was coordinated, in advance, with German authorities. Some claim that the West German government paid for the mission, wiring $5 million to the account of the PFLP for the simulated hijacking. When Ulrich Wagner, senior aide to the interior minister Genscher, was asked point-blank and on camera what he thought of the alleged German-Palestinian scheme, he replied, "Yes, I think it's probably true." One detail pointing to the likelihood of the scheme was the composition of the passengers: they were few, and they were all male. This unusual occurrence supports, but does not prove, the conspiracy theory.

Whatever the case, the Germans were guided by pragmatism rather than principle—and chose appeasement over confrontation. From the time of the Olympic massacre to the end of the 1980s, there was not a single armed Palestinian attack against Germans, despite Palestinian terrorist activity all over Europe. All the while the German secret service cultivated close ties with most of the Palestinian terror groups, including Fatah. Their main liaison was Atef Bseiso.

West Germany's speedy release of the Black September terrorists produced astonishment and rage in Israel. The Israeli ambassador was called back to Jerusalem for "consultations." Israel also promptly launched a retaliatory air raid against four Palestinian training camps in Syria, killing sixty-five people. *Time* magazine explained the reprisal as a move against Hafez Al-Assad's regime, one of the few that publicly harbored terrorists and financed their operations.

Golda Meir was in her office when she learned of the German decision to free the terrorists. "I was literally physically sickened," she wrote in her memoirs. Days later, when Zvi Zamir and Mike Harari came to her office seeking authorization to assassinate the PLO representative in Paris, she was quick to agree.

21 A RIPE TARGET

Mahamoud Hamshari, the PLO's unofficial man in Paris, was a soft target. His job demanded that he meet with anyone interested in discussing the "Palestinian cause." He had no bodyguard, no nervous tingling on the back of his neck, no instinct to look over his shoulder. He held a Ph.D. in history and espoused progressive political opinions in public. Though the Zu'aytir assassination sent ripples of fear through the Palestinian leadership in Europe, Hamshari thought his status as a quasi-diplomat made him immune from the Mossad's deadly reach.

Hamshari didn't think twice when an Italian journalist invited him for coffee. They met near his house at a corner café on the Left Bank. The journalist lobbed softball questions at the pudgy thirty-eight-year-old, who answered at great length in fluent French. After two hours of chitchat the two shook hands. Hamshari offered his card in case any follow-up questions should arise. He had no notion that the inquisitive journalist received his paycheck from Tel Aviv. The agent, an undercover operative from

Caesarea, had met with Hamshari to confirm his identity, address, and phone number. Over a cup of coffee, Hamshari had given the Mossad the verification they needed to plan his death.

Getting to Hamshari was relatively easy; executing him without harming his wife and child, while keeping the operatives' cover intact, was proving difficult. Although surveillance had followed his every move for the past two weeks, Harari and his staff officers had not been able to draft a solid plan. They knew they had to act promptly: soon Hamshari might catch an appraising stare or feel the heat of a tail.

Harari sought assistance outside his Caesarean empire. Although Harari hated the idea of bringing in outsiders, Zvi Zamir ordered him to summon Keshet—Rainbow, the Mossad's burglary unit, which specialized in covert breaking and entering into locked apartments, hotel rooms, safes, and factories. In 1972, Zvi Malchin commanded the tiny unit. Twelve years before, he had apprehended Adolf Eichmann on Garibaldi Street in Buenos Aires and brought him, drugged and without the sanction of international law, to an Israeli court for justice.

In those chaotic days the Mossad and Military Intelligence considered all PLO envoys a part of the terrorist infrastructure, believing that attacks were planned in their homes and offices. Quasi-diplomats from the Fatah wing of the PLO often transferred money, mail, and weapons to the armed wing of the party. Like the Jewish *saya'an*s the Mossad used around the world, these expatriated Palestinians didn't ask questions when their homeland called.

Hamshari was no different in this regard, but the Mossad also believed that he had played a role in the bombing of a Swiss Air flight on February 21, 1970, from Zurich to Tel Aviv, which took the lives of forty-seven passengers and crew. They also fingered him as an indirect accomplice to a PFLP plan to murder Israel's first prime minister, David Ben-Gurion, during a trip to Denmark in May 1969. Hamshari's apartment was allegedly used as an arms storehouse for Black September.

While Hamshari met with the "Italian journalist," a Keshet operative waited outside his apartment on Rue d'Alésia. With Hamshari's French wife, Marie-Claude, and their daughter, Amina, under surveillance and far from the home, the operative went to work. It was the second time he had entered Hamshari's home. A few days earlier he had broken in and snapped photos of the apartment from every conceivable angle. Caesarea's staff officers pored over the snapshots and decided that a small individual-sized bomb would be the best way to kill the historian. The photos showed that Hamshari worked at his desk. In the mornings, after his wife and child left home, he'd be alone. The operative stuck the thin slice of plastic explosive just under the telephone. The device was activated by a coded electronic signal, which a tiny antenna would pick up and forward to the electric detonator. All they needed was his voice on the phone to verify that he was in the apartment and five hundred meters of unobstructed access to the device.

After checking that everything was in place, the operative left the apartment. He left no sign of his presence.

The next day, Friday, December 8, in the early morning, a few minutes after 0800 hours, Marie-Claude headed out with Amina. In a command room not far away, Harari, Zamir, and several staff officers from headquarters waited. The Caesarea surveillance team had reported on Hamshari's personal habits. He usually crawled back into bed after his wife left for work. He didn't receive visitors, and the building was quiet late in the morning. The "journalist" dialed Hamshari's number. He got to the receiver on the third ring.

"Hello?"

"Can I please speak with Dr. Hamshari?"

"He is speaking," Hamshari said, in the formal French third person.

The Caesarea agent gave his partner an agreed-upon signal. The partner pressed the remote control, sending an electronic signal to the explosive device. The explosion crackled in the still Parisian morning. Hamshari was critically wounded, the apartment blown apart. Three weeks later Hamshari died in his hospital bed from massive internal injuries. Before his death he told investigators from the Paris police about the Italian reporter who called him seconds before the blast.

PLO leaders in Europe began to fear for their lives. The day after the assassination, Arab diplomats convened in Paris and publicly demanded that the French government assume responsibility for their well-being. At the end of the three-hour press conference, Fauzi Gariani, the senior Libyan representative in the city, bemoaned "the atmosphere of Zionist terror in France."

A steady trickle of news posthumously incriminated Zu'aytir and Hamshari. The sources were always "high-ranking officials" in Israeli intelligence. The deterrent effect was taking hold: Palestinian operatives, rather than planning their next high-profile attack, began to concentrate on their own survival.

• • •

By the end of 1972 Caesarea had expanded and evolved. Harari now had three assassination squads of roughly a dozen people each at his disposal. The teams had a basic structure, but were shaped to organically fit each individual mission. There were always three squads—logistics, surveillance, and assassination. The logistics squad rented apartments, drove the cars, spoke the local language, and was in charge of communications—a tedious chore in those days, involving complex codes. The surveillance team, frequently the largest, had many female members (who often acted as parts of "couples"). Their job was to blend into their surroundings. They employed very basic tactics, switching glasses, hats, wigs, and outerwear. As one former Caesarea combatant told me: "We were supposed to walk on the shadow of life." The final component of each group were the assassins. They were combatants trained in pairs and referred to as "number 1" and "number 2," generally well-prepared young men from top-flight army units.

All members of Caesarea led secret lives even within the Mossad. They were the most elite arm of Israel's defense forces, and they were reminded of this often. They were told that they were fulfilling the express wishes of the prime minister. The country was behind them.

As the Mossad's strength grew, so too did the Palestinians' ability to vanish. The chase intensified, becoming more complicated. Targets disappeared, swallowed by the earth.

Some claimed that Hamshari's assassination was carried out in a deliberately extravagant manner, strengthening the Mossad's deterrent message. In fact, the spy agency's goal was success and safety, not flash. "If I could take them down with a missile from twenty miles away, I would," an ex-Caesarea officer explained to me. "It isn't the method that's important, even if it is interesting and fascinating, it's the end result that counts. The goal was to intercept and prevent. We checked what he had done in the past, and what damage he could inflict in the future. We acted according to this analysis."

Chief of Staff Lieutenant General David Elazar spoke before the
Israel Defense College's graduating class on December 19, 1972,
nine days after Hamshari's assassination in Paris. The Mossad
never publicized its role in European assassinations, but Elazar
wanted to make a point. "Whoever reads the papers," he said,
"will see Arab hands involved in the death of a number of Arabs
in different countries. If you look closely, you will see the Jewish
thumbprint in the middle of the mix."

22 THE SLIPPERY SLOPE

Fatah wasn't flying the white flag. Their search for weak links in Israel's defenses took them to Thailand, where they found a vulnerable Israeli embassy. Months prior, the remote embassy had received new security directives, but the Thai pace of affairs, their distance from Europe, and the fact that Thailand was low on Israel's list of priorities all contributed to the laissez-faire security deployment at the embassy. On December 28, 1972, four armed Palestinians sent by Ali Hassan Salameh breezed past security and walked through a set of unlocked doors into the embassy's main hall. They took four Israeli men and two women hostage, throwing them into a third-floor room with their hands bound. The Israeli ambassador, Rechavam Amir, and his wife were not among them. The couple had gone out two hours earlier, to attend the coronation of Prince Maha Vajiralongkorn.

The terrorists floated their typewritten demands down to the Thai police waiting below. Black September demanded the release of thirty-six prisoners from Israeli jails. Their list included

Kozo Okamoto, serving a life sentence for his role in the Lod Airport attack one and a half years earlier, and Rimah Tanoos and Teresa Khalsa, the two surviving perpetrators of the foiled Sabena attack, both not yet one year into long prison sentences.

The Israeli ambassador returned to the besieged embassy in the company of the Thai prime minister, Thanom Kittikachorn; the Thai chief of staff; and several government ministers. The Thai leaders, all veterans of the armed forces, were enraged by the timing of the attack. Thailand was the only Southeast Asian country that had never been colonized. Their monarchs were still revered. A rolling coin with the likeness of the king was always picked up with a hand, never stopped with an unclean foot. The disruption of the coronation ceremony was a serious affront. The Thais and the Israeli ambassador (who had conducted a quick consultation with the Foreign Ministry in Jerusalem) were of one mind regarding the terrorists' demands—they would not capitulate.

The stalemate was broken by an unlikely source: Mustafa Issawi, the Egyptian ambassador. On directives from President Anwar Sadat, he took an active role in the thirty-hour negotiations with the terrorists. Issawi succeeded in convincing the terrorists to leave Thailand; their preliminary demands were unfulfilled, but two months later, as if disconnected, the Israeli government released several Palestinian corpses to Lebanon, as a gesture of "gratitude to Thailand." The four terrorists released the six Israeli hostages at the Bangkok airport and boarded a Thai plane to Egypt. The Egyptian ambassador flew with them, guaranteeing their safety with his presence as he had promised. As the Thai DC-8 flew to Cairo, five Israeli officers landed in Bangkok after twenty-four hours of travel. They were there to plan a rescue mission for an Israeli commando team that was on its way. Diplomatic negotiations allowing Sayeret Matkal commandos to operate in Thailand were ongoing. The Israeli government was ready to do all in its power to avoid another tragic end to a hostage situation.

The Black September attack on the Israeli embassy in Bangkok was quickly forgotten, both in Israel and abroad. The terrorists' surrender to the Egyptian pressure was surprising. In Beirut, Ali Hassan Salameh was enraged by the operation's failure. He wanted another attack that would put the Palestinian predicament back in the limelight, highlighting the importance of Fatah and Black September.

• • •

At Mossad headquarters, the search for assassination candidates continued at a frantic pace. A connection to Munich, direct or indirect, was not a prerequisite for consideration. At the time, many in the Mossad believed that those who preached violence were as bad as those who practiced or aided it; both were legitimate targets. In mid-January, Prime Minister Meir authorized another targeted killing, the third since Munich. Hussain Abu-Khair, thirty-six, the newly appointed PLO envoy to Nicosia, Cyprus, was sentenced to death. He too was a soft target: he lived in a hotel (he had been in Cyprus for two months but had yet to rent an apartment), had no weapon or bodyguard, and didn't seem to fear bodily harm. A Caesarea surveillance team trailed him for close to two weeks without seeing any security detail, or any attentiveness on his part. Apparently he didn't think he was important enough to warrant the attention of the Mossad.

Abu-Khair had served as Fatah liaison to the Soviet KGB. Since the late 1960s, Nicosia had been crawling with all kinds of cloak-and-dagger characters. No self-respecting spy agency dared to pass on sending an envoy to the region. Russian, American, East German, Spanish, British, Bulgarian, Syrian, Egyptian, Palestinian, and Israeli agents walked the streets of the shady capital. Many of them ran their Middle East missions from the island. Dodgy agents, traitors, double-dealers, backstabbers, and murderers played spy games on this sun-drenched island. Occasionally a bullet-riddled body would turn up. The Cypriot authorities chose not to interfere—which was, all nations tacitly acknowledged, the preferred response.

Abu-Khair returned to the Olympic Hotel on President Makarios Avenue just before midnight, January 25, 1973. He had no idea that one of Zvi Malchin's Keshet operatives had sneaked into his room and placed an explosive device beneath his bed. As was the case with Hamshari, this device could be remotely activated. A Caesarea combatant waited in a car outside the hotel for word from the surveillance team that the mark had entered his room. He saw Abu-Khair's light flick on and off. The combatant gave him a minute to grope for his bed in the dark and then flipped the switch. The ensuing explosion ripped the man apart. Harari, who had been supervising the mission from a nearby hotel room, left the country along with his staff officers and the assassination team; they were back in Israel within hours.

That morning, the telephone had woken Ankie Spitzer. An unidentified man ordered her to listen to the news at 10 o'clock.

"Who is it?" she asked.

"Never mind," he said. "This is for Andrei."

He hung up.

The news announced that a mysterious explosion had killed the Fatah representative in Nicosia. Ankie would receive more such calls in the future.

. . .

The following day, R., Caesarea's chief intelligence officer, opened a cabinet in his room on the eleventh floor of the Hadar Dafna Building. Inside was a row of photographs—Abu-Khair's was lined up just to the right of photos of Hamshari and Zu'aytir. R. drew an X through the photo of Abu-Khair. Harari watched R. work. We're on a roll, he thought. Many other photos sat propped to the left of Abu-Khair's. Who was next in line?

• • •

Individual Caesarea combatants executed missions. They were the ones the politicians alluded to when they waved their hands in the air, trumpeting Israel's ability to reach terrorists wherever they hid. But the aftershocks of Munich didn't affect only the people in the Mossad, Shabak, and Military Intelligence: it transformed the agencies themselves, their habits and their ability to cooperate. Before Munich, each intelligence agency operated on its own, in virtual isolation. Now heads of divisions, units, and wings understood that egos and institutional rivalries had to be cast aside in favor of interagency cooperation. Aharon Yariv, advisor to the prime minister on terrorism, worked tirelessly to smooth the rough patches and create a positive atmosphere during the many tense interagency meetings.

When a direct, underground line was laid between Military Intelligence's Branch 4 shacks and the Hadar Dafna Mossad Facha division—only three hundred yards away and, till then, a world apart—a breakthrough in cooperation was achieved. "It was a direct line, without operators or other barriers, which was also progress," a senior Military Intelligence source told me. "We also thought of computerizing our personnel files in an attempt to solve the four-sided problem of matching a name to a person. Every Arab name has four components: his first name, his father's name, his grandfather's name, and his clan name. If you catch a piece of information about a person, but all you have is a first name and sometimes also a family name, it might be impossible to find out who he is. Back then you couldn't cross-reference with the push of a button. It took endless research and thought to make a full name, but it was worth it because the name is the building block, the first step toward cracking a case. A full name led to many targets and operations. Back then we tried to computerize our personnel files but the technical problems were too great. We didn't do it, but the possibility of cooperation was something new and worthwhile."

The agencies were not ready for total cooperation, however. "In early 1973 I went to Aharon Yariv with a detailed plan to construct a command center, maybe we would call it 'Terror War Room,' " my source said. "It would be open twenty-four hours a day and it would serve and be run by all of the intelligence agencies. Yariv looked at me with those blue eyes and after a few beats of silence said, 'What you're proposing is totally impossible. We should make it happen, but we won't; we're not there yet.' "

Military Intelligence was used to anticipating war. They carefully watched army maneuvers and troop movements across the hostile countries to the north, east, and south. But after Munich Lieutenant Colonel Mor began issuing a weekly Hostile Terror Activity Report, known in Hebrew as Facha, an acronym that has become part of the everyday vocabulary. The weekly report went to the prime minister, the chief of staff, the defense minister, the head of Military Intelligence, the Shabak, and the Mossad. It included new alerts for pending terrorist attacks, statistics on terrorist activity, analysis of collected information, and, occasionally, a detailed indictment of suspected terrorists.

• • •

A senior intelligence source told me, "Our blood was boiling. Everything that pertained to terrorism was hot. We were on an assignment given to us directly by the prime minister. Sometimes pressure from the operational branches bent the will of the analysts. It's not that they said target X is worthless and we still decided to kill him, but when there was information implicating someone we didn't inspect it with a magnifying glass.

"You didn't need blood on your hands for us to assassinate you. If there was intelligence information, the target was reachable, and if there was an opportunity, we took it. As far as we were concerned we were creating deterrence, forcing them to crawl into a defensive shell and not plan offensive attacks against us. But in this field there is also a slippery slope. Sometimes decisions are made based on operational ease. It's not that the assassinated were innocent, but if a plan existed, and those were often easiest for the soft targets, you were condemned to death."

23 THE SHADOW WARS CONTINUE

Baruch Cohen, a talented *katsa,* arrived in Israel for a short visit in January 1973. He had been stationed in Brussels, Belgium, for the past two years. The risks he took working undercover left him frayed. A chance encounter with an old friend prompted him to reveal what had been weighing on his mind for months. "I die inside every time I think that my kids might grow up without their father." Two weeks later, on January 26, this father of four was killed in Madrid. One of his veteran sources, a Palestinian turncoat who had been "flipped" back by Black September, lured him to his death.

Baruch Cohen was thirty-six years old when he was killed. His family had lived in Haifa for five generations; he spoke Arabic with his parents and felt at ease in an Arab home. At twenty-three, one year after his army service, he joined the Shabak, working as a case officer in the field. He did his best work in Nablus's *casbah* and the surrounding refugee camps, eventually rising to the position of station chief. All the locals recognized him, calling him Captain. Tzomet requested his services in 1970, recognizing that beyond his natural talents as a charismatic and confidence-inspiring case officer, his familiarity with the territories and Palestinian life in general would help him recruit homesick students abroad.

The Palestinian cream of the crop was educated in Europe. There, the shock of the West brought insularity. Students shared apartments and dorms, shopped at the same stores, and hung out at the same nightclubs. Amidst the uncovered women and the bland food, they carved out their own world. For Fatah's Black September and the Marxist Palestinian terror organizations this was fertile ground for recruitment. The students who joined their ranks—often just looking for a familiar environment—were an integral part of Palestinian terror organizations' European infrastructures.

In 1972, there were approximately six thousand Palestinians in West Germany (out of 55,000 Arabs total), the majority of them students. The situation in Italy, France, Holland, Belgium, and Scandinavia was similar. One Palestinian agent, in an interview on September 25, 1972, in Beirut with James Bell of *Time* magazine, explained, "We are everywhere now. We are all over Western Europe, and there are many Palestinians among the 12,000 Arab students in the U.S. We have our own businesses like a diplomatic nightclub in Rome, which the authorities closed last April. But there are a lot more. There are travel agencies that can arrange things. There are laundries and grocery stores. But of course, these businesses are not solely businesses. They are also collection agencies, mail drops, meeting places, points of contact."

The Mossad fished from the same irresistible pond. While the Palestinian resistance groups used homesickness and patriotism as their lures, the Mossad baited with cash. Poor people were more likely to listen to an offer. Tzomet received a steady stream of information from the Shabak about the families of students pursuing degrees abroad. They knew which side of the law they were on; who their friends were; where they stood on nationalism and religion; and how much money their family had under the floorboards.

Cohen didn't stumble for words when he first approached a potential source. He would role-play for days, rehearsing dozens of possible scenarios. He would never introduce himself as an Israeli. A man would betray his homeland for the right reason, but giving information to a Zionist was the greatest possible treason. Cohen would say he worked for NATO or Spain or Egypt. He would inquire about the health of his target's family, asking specifically about an elderly relative. He would know if his target was gay, sex-starved, homesick, or in debt. He would find out if the person had a lifelong desire and then dangle it before his eyes. He would know if his mother was sick and offer a cure—perhaps admittance to a European hospital—in exchange for just a few short answers. He would have an abundance of Middle Eastern cakes and cookies on hand. He would play popular music. If he thought it would help relax his target, he would step out of a hotel room and a one-hundred-dollar-an-hour hooker would walk in. Baruch Cohen's job was to read and rule the mind of his source. All he wanted was to have a little talk.

In the summer of 1970 Cohen moved with his wife, Nurit, and his four children, the youngest of whom, Michal, was four, to Brussels. The Belgian capital was his base, but he traveled all across the continent. On light workweeks he would leave his family on Monday, returning on Friday for Sabbath. He spent time at the universities and cafés frequented by young Palestinians. There were other *katsa*s working parallel beats, artfully persuading individuals to betray their people, exposing themselves to immense risk.

Since Munich, Cohen and his peers in Tzomet were under pressure to recruit as many sources as possible. The gap between what was needed to create a map of Palestinian terrorism in Europe and what they knew was vast. There was no starker example than the Munich Massacre, a high-profile attack Israel knew nothing about. Fatah had been on the offensive since early 1972, striking hard and often at Israeli targets abroad. Their attacks were bold and aimed at Israel's weakest points. The HUMINT produced by Cohen and his peers was Israel's first line of defense. They were the ones charged with blocking the terrorists' advances. Despite the Mossad's assassination campaign, highly motivated terrorists were not—or not yet—in short supply. The only way to stop them was by foiling their plans through superior knowledge.

On the eve of his death, Cohen called his wife in Brussels and told her that he would be a day late. "I'll be back on Friday, before Shabbat, around six," he said. Nurit did not know where he was calling from, or what false name he was living under. After more than ten years of marriage to a man in the secret service she knew not to probe. Occasionally when he returned to Brussels, she would let curiosity get the better of her, and would ask where he had been. Cohen would grunt out the name of a place—London, Vienna, Berlin. She never went further, never asked: and what did you do there?

The next morning, in downtown Madrid, Cohen met Samir, a Palestinian student and Fatah activist he had cultivated as a reliable source, at Café Morrison, on Calle José Antonio. As they were leaving the café two men suddenly approached them. Cohen's informant broke into a run. Cohen understood what was happening, but had no time to react. Three quick rounds slammed into his chest. A fourth, errant bullet hit a pedestrian. Cohen collapsed on the sidewalk, in a pool of his own blood, his internal organs ruptured. The two gunmen escaped with the double agent. Passersby dispersed in a flash. The Madrid police arrived on the scene minutes later. An ambulance carried Cohen to the Francisco Franco Hospital, where he died on the operating table.

That evening Black September published a notice heralding the assassination of an Israeli Mossad agent by the name of Uri Molov. The Israeli passport Cohen carried in his pocket said Moshe Hanan Yishai. Initial media reports stated an Israeli citizen by that name had been murdered in Madrid. Since the state of Israel and Spain, under Generalissimo Francisco Franco, had no official ties, the Israelis preferred that Cohen's real name be kept secret. Only when the corpse was returned to Israel did the government publicize his identity. The prime minister's office issued an obituary for Cohen.

The media interpreted Cohen's murder as Black September's revenge for Zu'aytir, Hamshari, and Abu-Khair. The connection was coincidental. Black September's mission to assassinate Cohen had been devised months before. It was about feasibility, not retribution.

The officers at Tzomet headquarters in Tel Aviv were devastated. In the four months since the attempt on Tzadok Ofir's life, Tzomet had been scrambling to protect its officers abroad. Its plan called for each meeting between a *katsa* and his source, anywhere in the world, to be watched by a trained bodyguard. This logistically complex procedure would take a year to implement fully. Cohen fell between the cracks. His source, Samir, was considered reliable, which made their meeting a low priority.

The man who betrayed Cohen was put on the Mossad hit list and marked for death.

More than a decade later a Mossad officer tracked Samir down in Tunis. He walked past his house. The head of the Mossad at the time did not authorize his assassination. It was too risky.

24 ASSASSINATION IN KHARTOUM

Fatah had not lost sight of enemy number one—the Jordanian king and his regime. As Palestinian terror swept across Europe, Fatah officials in Beirut drafted an audacious plan to overthrow Jordan's King Hussein. The plan called for thirty-two terrorists—an unprecedented number—to storm the office of the Jordanian prime minister and take him and several government ministers hostage. Then they would booby-trap all the exits with explosives. With the hostages trapped and under their control, they would demand the release of one thousand of their compatriots rotting in Jordanian jails. The king would be ambushed and killed on his way to the exchange site. Abu-Daoud, the mastermind behind the Munich attack, was chosen by Abu-Iyad to command the mission. Their goal: to destabilize the Hashemite state and claim it as their own.

In February 1973, Abu-Daoud arrived in Amman, Jordan, carrying forged papers and dressed as a wealthy Saudi sheik. He was accompanied by a young woman posing as one of the rich sheik's wives. The Jordanian intelligence service, one of the world's best in gathering HUMINT, followed them closely from the moment they entered the country. Days later the pair were stopped at what seemed like a random roadblock. It was a trap. The two were taken into custody and interrogated immediately. A Jordanian intelligence source, a high-ranking Fatah member, had informed his handlers that Abu-Daoud was on his way to Jordan to case the prime minister's office.

Abu-Daoud broke under interrogation, revealing all the details of the planned coup. Abu-Daoud also spoke freely about the Munich attack, telling British TV reporters and Jordanian radio all about the perfectly planned strike. Black September was dealt a triple blow: not only had their most ambitious plan to date been thwarted, but an unidentified mole, somewhere in the upper echelons of their command structure, continued to operate, unobstructed. Fatah's Black September leaders in Beirut and Damascus felt like their every move was being watched by the Jordanians. In addition, their top operational guy was captured. At the close of a swift military trial Abu-Daoud was found guilty and sentenced to death.

Abu-Iyad, both friend and commander to Abu-Daoud, was prepared to do anything in his power to bring the Jordanian wheels of justice to a halt. He hastily planned and authorized a deadly attack. On the first of March, seven Palestinian terrorists, armed with AK-47s, grenades, and pistols, left Beirut for Khartoum, the capital of Sudan. Ten hours later, they stormed the Saudi embassy while the ambassador hosted a party for George C. Moore, the homeward-bound American deputy chief of mission. Guests poured out of the house, escaping through the garden as the terrorists charged through the front gate. Within minutes the group controlled the building. The commander of the raid sorted through the captives and kept only the most valuable: Cleo A. Noel, American ambassador to Sudan; George C. Moore; Guy Eid, the Belgian chargé d'affaires; and his Jordanian and Saudi counterparts.

The terrorists' list of demands was familiar: the Germans must release a number of Baader-Meinhof operatives; the Americans, Sirhan Sirhan, the Palestinian murderer of Robert F. Kennedy; the Israelis must free a host of prisoners, including the two women captured during the Sabena takeover; and, finally, the Jordanians were required to open the death row cell of Mohammed Oudeh, aka Abu-Daoud. If their demands were not met the hostages would be shot.

Golda Meir, King Hussein, and U.S. president Richard Nixon refused to bargain with the terrorists. Nixon delivered a televised address, announcing that the United States would not bow to extortion. Thirty-six hours later, without any prior communication, the terrorists rounded up the two U.S. diplomats and their Belgian counterpart and executed them in the basement of the embassy. Each man was shot dozens of times. Twenty-four hours later the terrorists released the two Arab diplomats and surrendered to Sudanese forces.

The tight timetable for the operation had taken its toll; Black September had made many uncharacteristic mistakes. The Sudanese president, Colonel Jaafar Numeiry, furious that an attack had taken place in his capital city, sent officers to comb through the PLO offices in Khartoum. They found that Fawwaz Yassin, the head of the PLO mission, had fled the country hours before the attack, leaving behind a sketch of the Saudi embassy that he himself had made. Further: an official PLO Land Rover had been used to drive the terrorists to the embassy, and the commander of the attack was in fact the PLO's number two man in Khartoum.

The investigation's findings—which were highly publicized—proved that Black September and Fatah were inextricably linked, that the former was merely an unofficial arm of the latter. Many branches of American and European intelligence agencies were forced to reckon with this uncomfortable fact after Khartoum. The Sudanese investigation also proved that PLO diplomats, contrary to beliefs widely held at the time, did not abstain from terror attacks and did not confine their area of operations to Israel and the Occupied Territories. They worked as *saya'an*s and were quite willing to dirty their hands for the cause. These revelations damaged Fatah's image abroad—they could no longer be seen simply as freedom fighters taking up arms solely against their Israeli occupiers. Killing unarmed diplomats in a basement did not play well in the international media. The week after the murder of the diplomats *Time* magazine published an article about the incident. It was titled "A Blacker September."

25 ANOTHER MAN DOWN IN PARIS

Dr. Basil Al-Kubaisi's file was one of the thickest in Caesarea's system. It was crammed with intelligence bulletins, evaluations, plans, memos, notes. A black-and-white photo of Al-Kubaisi in a dark suit hung inside chief intelligence officer R.'s cabinet. The Mossad had identified the man as a clever and evasive *saya'an*. Despite his role in lethal terror attacks, he remained a soft target: he visited European cities, had no security guard, and kept to a semipredictable routine. Several Caesarea surveillance teams had been trailing Al-Kubaisi since December 1972. He visited Paris regularly, in love with the City of Light. He would stay for a few days, take no obvious measures to avoid surveillance, and then vanish. Days later, the Facha division would learn from gathered intelligence that Al-Kubaisi was planning to return to Paris. The surveillance crews would be dispatched once again to trail him, only to be stymied yet again. The game of cat and (blithely unaware) mouse continued for three months. At the time it was one of Caesarea's longest ongoing missions.

Dr. Basil Al-Kubaisi, forty, had a perfectly manicured mustache and soft eyes. He looked incapable of committing the sorts of crimes the Mossad accused him of. An Iraqi, he was a left-wing law professor who believed in Pan-Arabism and sided with the Palestinian cause for ideological reasons. He was probably not affiliated with Fatah's Black September and certainly had no hand in the Munich Massacre. There was nothing extreme in his appearance; his clothes were fit for the academy, he was elegant and well kempt. But according to Branch 4 and the Mossad's intelligence, he helped the PFLP smuggle weapons and explosives for Western European terror attacks, slipping across borders and past customs officials without arousing suspicion. Raw intelligence data implied that his involvement in terrorism stretched back to the days of the Iraqi monarchy. In 1956, Al-Kubaisi was allegedly involved in a plot to kill King Faisal with a booby-trapped car, positioned along the king's route. A delay in the monarch's convoy saved the king's life, but forced Al-Kubaisi to flee Iraq. He made it to Beirut and from there to America and then Canada, where he received his doctorate in international law.

In 1971, Al-Kubaisi returned to the Middle East. Denied entry to his homeland, he took up residence in the then cosmopolitan hub of the Levant, Beirut, teaching law at the American University and affiliating himself with the PFLP. Various sources in the PFLP claimed that Al-Kubaisi was involved in the planning of a string of attacks along America's eastern seaboard. On March 6, 1973, Al-Kubaisi allegedly aided and assisted a PFLP team that placed a car packed with explosives close to the El Al terminal at New York's JFK Airport on the day that Golda Meir was due to land. The car was discovered before her arrival. Intelligence data also showed him to be a senior member of George Habash's PFLP and one of the planners of the attack at Lod Airport in 1972. Israeli Military Intelligence, the Mossad, and Aharon Yariv believed that the amassed intelligence before them warranted

Al-Kubaisi's death. He had a terrorist past, a terrorist present, and in all likelihood a terrorist future. All agreed that liquidating the talented *saya'an* would prevent future attacks and send the required message to those devoted to the terrorist cause. It was time for him to meet his maker. Prime Minister Golda Meir and the defense cabinet authorized the mission.

In early April 1973, Caesarea's surveillance crews caught up with Al-Kubaisi in a small Parisian hotel adjacent to the lovely Madeleine Church. The surveillance teams had studied his daily routine, recording his every move, and Caesarea's "Senate," their forward command center in Europe, had rushed to complete an assassination plan. After seven months of intensive action in the field, Caesarea's surveillance and hit teams were in good form—professional and quick. Their hands-on experience kept the tension low and their guard up at all times. The mission was set for April 6. Mike Harari and Zvi Zamir arrived in Paris that afternoon, heading straight to their command room in a Mossad safe house. All the preparations had been made; all remaining decisions were in the hands of the two assassins and the one field commander closing in on Al-Kubaisi.

At sunset, the surveillance crew reported that the subject had finished eating at the upscale Café de la Paix. He left the restaurant, bought a newspaper, and began walking toward his hotel, down one of the side streets next to the Madeleine Church. Al-Kubaisi made a detour, spending close to an hour with a local prostitute. When he emerged, two assassins approached him, rapidly closing the gap between them. Al-Kubaisi had time to yell, in French, "*Non, ne faites pas cela!* No, don't do this!" before they opened fire, shooting him nine times from close range with their silenced Beretta 0.22 pistols. Al-Kubaisi collapsed in front of the corner pharmacy, dying alone on Paris's Rue Chauveau Lagarde.

George Habash's PFLP published a death announcement for Dr. Basil Al-Kubaisi, declaring him a *shahid,* his murder a Zionist crime committed by Israeli intelligence. The announcement also blamed French authorities for their complicity in allowing the Zionists to operate unhindered on French soil. "This type of behavior on the part of the French authorities forces us to see the French government as collaborators with extremists, who operate against the interests of the Palestinian nation," it proclaimed. A search of Al-Kubaisi's hotel room turned up nine different passports and $1,000 in foreign currency. Harari's three assassination teams had now knocked off four Palestinians—second- and third-tier Fatah members, suspected *saya'an*s of Black September and the PFLP.

• • •

Mike Harari's safe in Caesarea's Tel Aviv headquarters contained a list with at least a dozen names on it. All were terrorists suspected of involvement in the Munich Massacre or other devastating attacks and included Palestinian leaders such as: Abu-Iyad, Fatah's second in command; Abu-Daoud, the architect of the Munich Massacre; Fakhri Al-Omri and Atef Bseiso, Abu-Iyad's operations officers; and, last but not least, Ali Hassan Salameh, a senior commander of Fatah.

Seven months after the Munich Massacre the priorities of Israel's intelligence agencies were firmly fixed. Their primary task was to warn of imminent attacks against Israeli targets in Europe and Israel. Their secondary priority was to supply field teams with the operational intelligence needed to plan and execute assassination missions. The intelligence poured in, but information pertaining to the men on the hit list remained weak and unreliable. Branch 4 and the Mossad's Facha division were still groping in the dark, but a massive effort to draft a HUMINT source within Black September was under way. It was clear to all that just one source could turn the tide.

The blacklisted men knew they were being hunted by Israel. Prime Minister Meir had declared as much from the Knesset's podium. Abu-Iyad and his comrades and Ali Hassan Salameh had to be protected, careful, alert, and armed to the teeth if they were to survive. Most of them feared leaving Beirut, where they felt relatively safe.

26 OPERATION SPRING OF YOUTH

Major Amnon Biran, Sayeret Matkal's chief intelligence officer, put on an overcoat and climbed to the deck of the Israeli missile boat *Ga'ash*. The cold, wind-driven salt spray stung his face as he stared across the water at the twinkling lights of Beirut two miles away. Sixteen commandos were on the ground, operating deep in enemy territory. Neither he nor any of the senior officers on board had heard a word from them in over fifteen minutes. They had slipped off sleek rubber boats on a Lebanese beach, radioed in their first codeword, and then gone silent.

The Sayeret Matkal commandos planned to assassinate three top-level Fatah officers in their bedrooms, in the heart of Beirut. It was Israel's most audacious counterterrorism mission to date. The intended message: "Our reach is long. We can find you any-where." The motive: deterrence, prevention, revenge.

The view from the ship's deck was grim. Major Biran paced the confined space, alternating his gaze between the waves and the bright lights of the city. Months of poring over maps and ae-rial photographs had helped him pinpoint a certain cluster of lights in the northwest corner of the city—in a few minutes the force should be there. But the silence irked him. They should have radioed in several codewords by now, signaling their advance through the city. Suddenly a trail of tracers cut through the night. He took a deep breath of concern: at least the teams had reached the right area. But why the tracer fire? Were they engaged in a firefight with the Lebanese army? His discomfort intensified.

The three targeted men were Muhammad Yussef Najar, forty-four, one of the founders and the current second in command of Fatah, known as Abu-Yussef, and a lawyer by training; Kamal Adwan, thirty-eight, a petroleum engineer and commander of the relatively new Western Wing, the Fatah division charged with attacks on Israeli soil; and Kamal Nasser, forty-eight, a Palestinian Christian who served as the PLO's chief spokesman. A talented poet, he was both charismatic and popular. The three lived next to one another, in two tall buildings in northwest Beirut, in the a-Sir neighborhood.

Abu-Yussef and Adwan were tied to terrorist operations against Israel since 1968. Several loose, uncorroborated strands of information even linked the two of them with Black September and the Munich attack. Undoubtedly, both were up to their necks in terrorist activity. Their planned assassination was mostly preventive in nature. The necessity and legitimacy of targeting the third man, Kamal Nasser, the spokesman, was debated for weeks. In the end, he was sentenced to death because Military Intelligence considered him an ideologue who sanctified and promoted the killing of innocent Israelis—and because the PLO lacked a clear distinction between its political and operational branches. According to Military Intelligence, the PLO's political activists, primarily in Europe, assisted terror attacks. They were legitimate targets.

Lieutenant Colonel Ehud Barak, future prime minister of Israel, commander of Sayeret Matkal at the time, led his men toward their targets in West Beirut. Over the past two years, he had been pushing the brass for more counterterrorism operations. The different elite forces of the IDF were all steeped in an unspoken yet competitive race to see who could pull off the most daring operation. This one began on a small pad of paper. Barak heard rumors in early 1973 that the IDF's Joint Chiefs were considering a mission deep in Beirut. He sent Major Biran to find out more. Biran poked around his contacts at the Mossad and learned that the brass was looking to locate several top-level Fatah targets in the Lebanese capital. A Mossad officer ripped a piece of paper out of a notepad and sketched the location of the homes of Abu-Yussef, Kamal Adwan, and Kamal Nasser. For Sayeret Matkal, known in Israel simply as the Unit, that was how the mission began.

In early February, Barak called his senior officers to a meeting. Yoni Netanyahu, older brother to future prime minister Benjamin Netanyahu and deputy commander of the Unit at the time, sat next to Major Muki Betzer, Major Biran, and Lieutenant Amitai Nachmani. The five of them looked closely at the black and white photos of Abu-Yussef, Kamal Nasser, and Kamal Adwan. Major Biran recited the terrorist biographies of the three, as he had received them from above. He unfurled an aerial map of Beirut. "Here," he said, pointing to the a-Sir neighborhood, "on Vardun Street, just beyond the American and British embassies and the luxury seaside hotels, in these two tall buildings." Everyone clustered around the map. There wasn't much to say. A lot of intelligence work had to be done before they could start on an operational plan.

Since the "Black September" of 1970, when Jordan's King Hussein's forces killed thousands of Palestinians and forced the survivors to flee, Beirut had become the home of many Palestinian terrorist organizations. Thousands of operatives from Fatah, and the left-wing organizations of George Habash, Naif Hawat-meh, and Ahmed Jibril, freely roamed the streets of the Lebanese capital. Neither their threat to Lebanese sovereignty nor the rule of law made much impression on them: weapons were slung casually over their shoulders. Outside their offices, where terrorist operations in Europe and Israel were planned, heavily fortified guard positions were set up, with machine guns and concrete blocks.

The Palestinians were not Beirut's only guests. The city had become a mecca of sorts for mostly left-wing international terror organizations. The West German Baader-Meinhof Gang, the Italian Red Brigades, the ASALA, and the Japanese Red Army all had scores of operatives in the city. They attended training camps and seminars. They were all part of a bizarre metropolis where bars and casinos stayed open all night, girls in bathing suits sunbathed on the beach, muezzins summoned the faithful to prayer five times a day, and terrorists gathered in alleyways.

Beirut was a factory for terrorism. The Sabena, Lod, Bangkok, and Munich attacks had been planned and supervised from high-rise apartments in the high-income areas of the city. Organization heads wove intricate attack plans and did not hide their activities.

Operation Spring of Youth began with Caesarea. The Mossad unit's combatants went into the field early, undercover, to collect intelligence for the Unit. They photographed the apartment buildings, filmed the street at all hours of the day and night, checked the traffic routes to and from the buildings, and observed everyday life in the neighborhood. The hundreds of hours of surveillance work would hopefully translate into half an hour of meticulously executed action.

The first question planners needed to answer: how to transport Barak's troops to Beirut, a one-million-person coastal city seventy-five miles north of Israel's border? Helicopters were ruled out almost immediately as too overt and dangerous. The sea proved a better option. Major Muki Betzer boarded an Israeli navy submarine to reconnoiter a five-mile stretch of beach along Beirut's south shore.

Biran pinpointed the beach of the Sands Hotel as a workable landing spot for the team. The benefit of landing on a private beach was obvious—no camping, no couples, and no fishermen. The downside was that the better rooms had balconies overlooking the sea. A late night cigarette on the balcony could lead to disaster. Caesarea's combatants observed the beachfront hotel for many nights and found that the chilly March winds, carrying grains of salt and sand, kept the hotel guests inside at night. The balconies were empty, the blinds drawn. Biran knew he could proceed.

The reports arrived in a steady stream. Caesarea's undercover combatants learned the layout of the lobby, the design of the staircases, and the number of stairs on each landing. They checked the schedule of the concierge to see when he would likely be at his post. They reported back to Tel Aviv how many guards typically manned the front doors. Biran investigated the Beirut police: how many policemen were on night duty across the city, how many would respond to a call in that part of town, with how many vehicles, in what time frame, and with what degree of professionalism.

The plan was remarkable. The chosen commandos would sail to Beirut on missile boats. Two miles offshore they would transfer to the naval commandos' Mark 7 rubber rafts, which would silently slide onto the shore. Three Caesarea reserves officers, posing as Canadian and European tourists, would wait in large American cars in the hotel's parking lot, their five-mile route committed to memory. "Our intention," said Major Betzer, deputy commander of the mission, "was to finish the mission as quickly as possible and avoid a small war in the streets of Beirut."

Betzer had been carrying a small, passport-size picture in his shirt pocket for the two weeks prior to the mission. Biran had given him the photo. He studied the lean face of Abu-Yussef at every opportunity—when all hell broke loose in the apartment, amidst the screaming and the sting of sweat in his eyes, he would recognize his target immediately. Once he'd pulled the trigger he would have one more opportunity to verify his target: Abu-Yussef was missing the pinkie finger of his left hand. The others carried similar photos.

The Unit's top fifteen commandos were picked for the mission. A sixteenth, Yoni Netanyahu (who would be killed three years later leading the daring rescue mission at Entebbe), joined at the last minute. Their practice drills mirrored the real thing. They got into rubber boats, motored to shore, docked, piled into cars, sat in their exact positions, and drove for five miles. They unloaded at two high-rise buildings in north Tel Aviv. The neighborhood was still under construction and had been commandeered at night by the army under false pretenses. The warriors split into four teams. Three went up to their assigned apartments, and one, under the command of Barak, remained on the street as a forward command center. They practiced the quick entry steps into the lobby and then watched one another's backs in a coordinated dancelike sprint up winding flights of stairs, guns aimed upwards, counting the floors as they climbed. Kamal Adwan lived on the second floor, Kamal Nasser on the third, and Abu-Yussef on the sixth floor of the neighboring building.

Lieutenant General David Elazar, the IDF chief of staff, came to observe the team's drills in north Tel Aviv. After watching a full rehearsal, he pulled Barak aside. "Look, Ehud," he said, "it doesn't look good. You guys will be tourists in civilian clothes, but all these men, at one-thirty in the morning? Their security guards are going to notice you guys, it's too suspicious . . . think of something else."

Barak, and Betzer, who was listening in, knew he was correct. It didn't look right. Elazar leaned in and said, "What if some of you came dressed as women?" Betzer liked the idea immediately. He turned to Barak and said, "Yeah, Ehud, let's dress up as couples. We'll walk spread out in pairs."

Betzer set himself to the task. The shortest warriors would wear the drag. Barak would be the hot brunette, Lonny Rafael and Amiram Levine, a future IDF general and deputy head of the Mossad, would be blondes.

The warriors carried all their weapons and explosives under their jackets and on their belts, or, in the case of the "ladies," in their fashionable purses and under their brassieres. During another dry run, Muki Betzer, a broad-shouldered man in a suit two sizes too big for him, walked hand in hand with Barak, the brunette, to the entrance of the building. Afterward Lieutenant General Elazar approached Betzer and felt his jacket, asking, "What do you have on under here?"

"Four grenades on my belt, an Ingram submachine gun under one arm, a Beretta under the other arm, and eight magazines, with thirty bullets each in these pockets," Betzer replied, showing an array of tailored pockets sewn into his suit. Elazar nodded.

Each warrior understood that if something went wrong with the plan, they were alone. No cavalry would come to Beirut. One night, after a long day of practice, Betzer gathered the three other men in his team. "We're going on an unusual mission, in the heart of a bustling city. There'll be guards at the doors to the place. The terrorists will be armed. There'll be lots of unarmed civilians around us. What we need to focus on is Najar; he needs to pay for his sins." Betzer paused. "If we do as we've planned, we'll leave the city in one piece. It's true, anything could happen, but we'll stay calm, confident, and clearheaded. Each problem has a solution." Finally, feeling he needed to hammer home the point of the mission, Betzer added: "This is the first time we are attacking an enemy with a name, not some unknown adversary with a weapon. As far as the state of Israel is concerned, these three guys have committed war crimes. This is revenge for Munich. We need them to feel our anger, and to fear us."

Three days before the mission began the entire Fatah leadership met in Kamal Nasser's apartment. Abu-Iyad, who years later revealed the meeting, noticed that there was no security outside the apartments of Abu-Yussef, Kamal Adwan, and Kamal Nasser. "You guys aren't cautious enough; an Israeli helicopter is going to land here someday soon and kidnap you," he said. All of them laughed, except for the preternaturally suspicious Arafat, who told them to hire security guards immediately. The night before the mission began, Abu-Iyad, the architect of Munich, slept not for the first time on Kamal Nasser's couch.

Late Monday morning, April 9, the Unit's sixteen warriors rolled up to the Haifa harbor on a bus packed with gear and weapons. IDF Chief of Staff Elazar and head of Military Intelligence Eli Zeira were waiting for them at the entrance to the harbor. They hopped on the bus and wished the fighters well. "All of a sudden I heard the Chief of Staff say 'Kill the bastards,' " remembers Betzer. "None of us thought the terrorists would throw their hands in the air and surrender, but we practiced catching them, cuffing them, and transporting them to Israel. Deep down inside we knew that the chances of bringing them back as prisoners were slim and that in truth the brass didn't really intend for us to do that, but the Chief of Staff's utterance was more explicit than usual."

The plan had evolved. Sayeret Matkal was no longer acting alone in Beirut. Their target was still the primary objective, but it was not the only one. The Chief of Staff and other intelligence officers figured that they would get one chance to strike in the heart of Beirut before terror organizations fortified their positions, rendering Israeli counterterror raids too dangerous. Spring of Youth had to be a one-hit wonder. Additional forces, paratroopers and naval commandos, would strike other terrorist targets. The first paratrooper team, led by Lieutenant Colonel Amnon Shahak, the commander of Battalion 50 and later the IDF's chief of staff and a government minister, was to strike a seven-story building in west Beirut, where dozens of terrorists from Naif Hawatmeh's Democratic Front for the Liberation of Palestine (DFLP) resided. The second additional target, a building in northern Lebanon, was suspected of serving as a demolitions factory, and was to be blown up by a paratrooper force under the command of Lieutenant Colonel Shmuel Firsburger. The final target, a suspected weapons factory, was to be detonated by Colonel Shaul Ziv, the commander of Shayetet 13, the naval commandos. Colonel Emanuel "Mano" Shaked, chief infantry and paratroops officer, was the commander of this part of the mission.

Before the raid was set into motion, the chief of staff approached Mano and shook his hand. "You believe in God?" he asked.

"That question pisses me off," Mano responded.

"Start praying anyway, because he'll be the only one who can help you," the chief of staff said, smiling. He winked and left.

The sea was smooth as pool water on the afternoon the forces set sail. The missile boats motored west, toward Cyprus, and then casually slipped into the shipping lane between Cyprus and Beirut. Time crawled. At midnight each force disembarked at its destination. The team from Sayeret Matkal jumped into naval commando black rubber boats, wearing plastic ponchos over their wigs and jackets. Several hundred yards from the shore the naval commandos cut the engines and began to paddle. They moved fast, in unison, in silence. As they approached the Sands Hotel beach the commandos slipped over the side and helped the passengers ashore. They hit the beach with dry feet and dry wigs.

Three rented Buick Skylarks waited in the parking lot. Mossad combatants, disguised as tourists, were at the wheel. All sixteen of the Unit's men squeezed into the cars and set off. The man behind the wheel of the lead car told Barak and Betzer that shortly before he had noticed a pair of Lebanese policemen loitering around the target area. Barak did not outwardly respond, nor did he radio this significant development back to the command center on the missile boat, fearing they would order him to abort the mission. Had he tried, he would have quickly discovered he was unable to transmit. The army signals radio was damaged when the team jammed into the car. Major Biran would worry in silence.

The cars joined Beirut's smooth nighttime traffic. They covered five northbound miles on the turnpike in twenty uneventful minutes. Around the corner from Vardun Street they piled out. It was 0130. The Mossad combatants, many of whom held regular civilian jobs and simply made themselves available for "assignments," drove down the street and parked, ready to assist at a moment's notice. They got out of their cars and spoke quietly among themselves, casually leaning on the hood and chatting.

Barak and Betzer led their team, walking arm in arm. Two policemen brushed past without giving them a second look. They split, each to his own target. The "brunette," Barak, stayed downstairs with the "blonde," Amiram Levine; the Unit's doctor, Shmuel Katz; and one naval commando. Betzer led three warriors through the lobby and up the stairs at a silent gallop. They stopped on the sixth floor and stuck explosives beneath the knob of Abu-Yussef's door. Betzer squeezed the rubber transmit button three times, signaling to Barak that he was ready to go. Each team would transmit an identical signal. When all were in place,

Future Prime Minister Ehud Barak, in white jumpsuit, releasing hostages from Sabena Flight 571 at Lod Airport, May 1972. *Photo courtesy GPO.*

A happy group photograph, taken just days before the Black September attack, of most of the members of the 1972 Israeli Olympic Squad.

1) Shaul Ladany, athlete; 2) Shmuel Lalkin, head of the delegation; 3) Kehat Shorr, marksman; 4) Mark Slavin, wrestler; 5) Zelig Shtroch, marksman; 6) Andrei Spitzer, fencing coach; 7) Esther Shachmorov, hurdler/sprinter; 8) Yitzhak Caspi, deputy leader; 9) Dan Alon, fencer; 10) Gad Tsabari, wrestler; 11) Eliezer Halfin, wrestler; 12) Shlomit Nir, swimmer; 13) Henry Hershkowitz, marksman; 14) Yitzhak Fuchs, team chairman; 15) Yossef Romano, weight lifter; 16) Dr. Kurt Weil; 17) Amitzur Shapira, athletics coach; 18) Tuvia Skolsky, weight lifting coach; 19) Ze'ev Friedman, weight lifter; 20) Yaakov Springer, weight lifting judge; 21) David Berger, weight lifter; 22) Moshe Weinberg, wrestling coach

The Israeli Olympic team parades in Olympic Stadium, Munich, August 26, 1972, during the opening ceremony. *Photo courtesy Associated Press.*

A member of the Black September commando group is seen wearing a hood on the balcony of the building where they are keeping the hostages. *Photo courtesy Associated Press.*

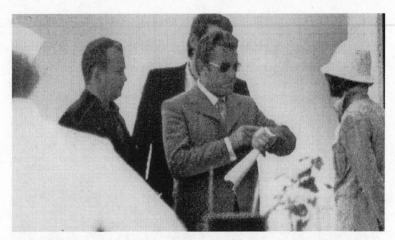

Dr. Manfred Schreiber, Munich's chief of police, looks at his watch while discussing the deadline with Issa, at right, outside the Israeli living quarters in the Olympic Village. The two men in the background are plainclothes police. *Photo courtesy Associated Press.*

Tony, second in command of the terrorists, leans out of a window to talk to Issa during negotiations with police chief Schreiber, far left, and West German interior minister Hans-Dietrich Genscher outside the Olympic Village residence in Connollystrasse 31. *Photo courtesy Associated Press.*

German police, armed with submachine guns and dressed in unassuming tracksuits, climb onto the roof of the building where the Israeli athletes are being held. *Photo courtesy Associated Press.*

Ankie Spitzer, widow of the slain Israeli fencing coach Andrei Spitzer, surveys the room at Munich's Olympic Village where her husband was held. Chalk outlines made by German police trace the impact of bullets. *Photo courtesy Associated Press.*

The two West German helicopters that carried the armed terrorists and their nine Olympian hostages pictured at Fürstenfeld-bruck air force base outside of Munich. The helicopter in the foreground is burned out as a result of a hand grenade set off by one of the terrorists. Nine of the eleven hostages were killed in the shootout at the air base. Five terrorists and one German policeman also died. *Photo courtesy Associated Press.*

Israeli Prime Minister Golda Meir addressing the Knesset. *Photo courtesy GPO.*

Aharon Yariv, the head of Military Intelligence until October 1972 when he became advisor on terrorism under Prime Minister Golda Meir. *Photo courtesy GPO.*

Three surviving terrorists from Munich at a press conference upon their release in Libya. From left to right: Adnan Al-Jishey, Jamal Al-Jishey, and Mohammed Safady. *Photo courtesy Getty Images.*

Then Chairman Yasar Arafat and Kamal Nasser are pictured here engaged in conversation prior to a meeting of the Executive Committee of the Palestine Liberation Organization, in Cairo, on February 27, 1971. *Photo courtesy Associated Press.*

Salah Khalaf (Abu Iyad), considered a major leader of Fatah, was the mastermind of the Munich attack. *Photo courtesy Palestinian Academic Society for the Study of International Affairs.*

Ali Hassan Salameh, one of Yasser Arafat's confidantes and the head of Force 17 in Fatah. He was killed by an Israeli-initiated car bomb on January 22, 1979, in Beirut. *Photo courtesy Palestinian Academic Society for the Study of International Affairs.*

Abu-Daoud (center), who claimed responsibility for the terrorist attack on Israeli athletes in Munich, is pictured here being escorted by French police at Paris's Orly Airport, January 11, 1977. *Photo courtesy AFP/Getty Images.*

Barak would activate the coordinated attack with five scratchy transmissions from his own, internal radio system. Betzer counted them out with his fingers, clenching his fist on the fifth. A second member of the squad flipped the switch on the activation device. Several seconds of silence ticked by. Suddenly the sharp popping sound of gunfire rose from the street. Two more seconds passed before the detonation device exploded, blowing the door off its hinges and filling the hall with smoke. Betzer and another commando stormed in. They knew the layout from the endless drills and simulations. Running down the hall toward the workroom, Betzer saw a familiar face peek out of the bedroom. He raised his Uzi at Abu-Yussef, the man whose picture he had kept in his breast pocket. The PLO activist slammed the door shut. Betzer unleashed a long blast of fire and then kicked it in. Both commandos found Abu-Yussef dead in a pool of blood, his fatally injured wife by his side. Betzer, worried by the shooting in the street, decided not to pick up Abu-Yussef's papers as planned, despite the waterproof bags they carried for that express purpose. He commanded his soldiers to follow him to the street below.

The other two teams were similarly successful. The spokesman, Kamal Nasser, was caught by surprise, sitting at his desk, in his pajamas, working on a eulogy for a friend. He ducked beneath the desk, opened fire, and hit one of the commandos in the leg. The second soldier through the door shot Nasser dead. The third target, Kamal Adwan, died in front of his wife and kids, a cold AK-47 in his hand. The soldiers shoved piles of paper into the bags and left the apartment within two minutes. Racing down the stairs, an apartment door opened, triggering immediate fire from the tense commandos. A seventy-year-old Italian woman, investigating the nighttime noise and commotion, was killed.

They raced out of the house; a firefight was in progress. Barak and Levine, in wigs and makeup, had been standing next to the doctor and naval commando when a curious security guard got out of a parked sedan and approached them. Crossing the street, he pulled out his weapon. Barak and Levine waited until he was a few yards away, drew their silenced pistols, and fired. The security guard retreated to his car, firing over his shoulder. Barak and Levine returned fire with their stock-less Uzis. A stray bullet activated the horn of the car, waking the neighbors, and probably prompting them to call the police, who would arrive with shocking alacrity. This gun battle is what Major Biran saw from the deck of the missile boat.

Once the security guard stopped firing, Barak summoned the getaway cars. As they pulled to a stop, a police Land Rover turned onto Vardun Street. Betzer tossed a grenade onto the canvas roof of the vehicle. Everyone inside was killed or maimed in the explosion. The soldiers squeezed back into the Buicks and raced toward the beach, tires squealing. The last car sprayed Ninja spikes behind them to impede any followers. Once they had slid back into the main artery of traffic, the drivers resumed a casual pace, arousing no suspicion. They parked on the seaside promenade, left the keys in the ignition, and went down to the water.

The naval commando from Barak's team signaled his buddies in the rubber Zodiacs waiting offshore. Their affirmation of the transmission was the first sign of life Biran and the other staff officers at the command center had heard since the teams had left the missile boat. They still had no idea whether the mission was a success, whether there were dead or injured; but they knew they were back. Biran breathed a sigh of relief. The thirty longest minutes of his life were over.

Boarding the missile boats, they were updated about the other components of the mission. Shahak's force, also in civilian garb and escorted by Mossad combatant drivers, had been engaged in a fierce firefight in front of the DFLP building. Two soldiers were killed, one critically injured. The forward entry team was able to lay the explosive devices under heavy fire and damage the building. Lieutenant Colonel Amnon Shahak would be awarded a citation for valor for his command under fire. The naval commandos and the paratroopers encountered no resistance, but, due to faulty intelligence, also found no weapons or demolitions factories.

The Israeli force returned to Haifa in the early morning hours. Chief of Staff Elazar received them. "Israel won't play by the rules of partial war; wars are not won with a strong defense," he said later to journalists.

Spring of Youth made a searing impression in the Arab world, a combination of anger, embarrassment, and awe. In Lebanon, the government collapsed in the aftermath of the attack. Lebanese newspapers published eyewitness accounts of two beautiful women—one a blonde, one a brunette—fighting like armed dervishes in the streets of Beirut, keeping police, army, and Palestinian operatives at bay with long bursts of automatic fire. Stories abounded. Myths grew. Israel's message of deterrence spread—the Mossad and the Israelis can reach anyone, anywhere, even in their bedrooms. Many contend that Spring of Youth resonated more powerfully than any of the Mossad's previous missions in Europe.

Half a million people attended the funerals. The top-level PLO and Fatah officials were deeply alarmed. Their lives were suddenly in peril. According to Abu-Iyad, Arafat was in one of the adjacent buildings that night. Both he and Abu-Iyad felt at home in the three dead PLO officials' homes. It was perfectly conceivable that Arafat and Abu-Iyad could have gone up to their friends' apartments for coffee or dinner following the PLO Central Committee convention held the night of the raid. Ali Hassan Salameh was home that night too. He lived two hundred yards from where Barak and Levine stood.

Years later Abu-Iyad wrote in *Stateless* that he had asked to sleep at Kamal Nasser's house that night. The bachelor turned him down, explaining that he had to write his eulogy for the poet friend. Abu-Iyad writes that he left dejectedly. Instead of spending the night with the charismatic spokesman, he went to the apartment of the three Munich "survivors," to hear stories of their "adventures." He and one of his assistants, Tirawi, went up to the hide-out apartment of the Munich "survivors" at 2130 hours.

"All of a sudden I heard shots. . . . The increasing fire, accompanied by loud booms, made me suspicious. . . . And then the doorman ran into the apartment and cried out in a garbled voice: 'Al-Yahud, al-Yahud, the Jews are here!' He was shaking uncontrollably, unable to say another word. The prophecy I voiced a few days earlier without much conviction nearly came true. The Israelis were at our doors, plain and simple."

The myth of Israel's military capacity and the long reach of the Mossad was hitting its peak. Built largely on the assassinations in Europe, it became truly formidable after Operation Spring of Youth, remembered by Palestinians as "Amaliyat Vardun," Vardun Mission, an enduring testament of the Israeli intelligence agencies' ability to strike anywhere on the planet.

27 EUROPE'S INDIFFERENCE

Spring of Youth did not demand Caesarea's full attention. While that operation was in motion, two more were under way. The first was a soft target in Nicosia, Cyprus; the second, a slightly more difficult man to reach, in a hotel in Athens, Greece.

On the evening of April 9, Caesarea combatants, with the help of a Keshet specialist, laid an explosive device under the hotel bed of Ziad Mokhsi. Mokhsi, the PLO representative in Cyprus, replaced Hussain Abu-Khair, who had been killed by the Mossad more than two months prior. Mokhsi died instantly. R., Caesarea's chief intelligence officer, could open the cabinet in his office and draw another black X.

It seems, however, that Ziad Mokhsi had no connection to Munich. The assassination fit the rule of deterrence, but Mokhsi's primary sin was his vulnerability. Israeli intelligence agencies interpreted his death sentence differently, of course. To them, he deserved to be added to the list because of his work as a PLO representative, which often entailed assisting in the preparatory stages of Fatah attacks against Israel and its citizens. As fate would have it, two amateurish terror attacks failed on the very day of his death. The Libyan-backed National Arab Youth Organization attempted to attack the Israeli ambassador's house in Nicosia, and to hijack an Israeli Arkia Airlines plane on the runway.

Moussa Abu-Zaiad, one of Salameh's operatives, came to Athens planning to execute a major terror attack. A tough target, Abu-Zaiad behaved as if he were in enemy territory in Athens. He rarely left his room in the Aristides Hotel and forbade house-keeping from entering. "He looked preoccupied," one hotel worker remarked. On April 9, he sent a cable to a post office box in Beirut: "If you would like the job to be done right, you had best come over here."

On his way to the port of Piraeus near Athens he went to great lengths to shake any possible tail, switching cabs in the middle of his trip, taking many side streets, and paying careful attention to his back. Caesarea combatants followed him throughout. After a few days of surveillance, the commander of the mission decided that the best way to end Abu-Zaiad's life without jeopardizing safety or cover was to plant an explosive device in his room. All they needed was Zamir's approval before picking the appropriate time and place.

Spring of Youth shook Abu-Zaiad from his precautionary routine. He had heard snippets of information about the stunning mission that ended the lives of numerous senior Fatah activists, but was still unable to piece together the full story. He finally left his room to buy a newspaper. The commander of the assassination team sent a surveillance crew to follow him, and, if necessary, detain him, until the Keshet burglary operative and the Caesarea combatant finished attaching a bomb under his hotel room bed. Abu-Zaiad hurried to a nearby newspaper stand, bought a few papers with screaming headlines about the raid in Beirut, and returned to his room. He left the Mossad operatives little time to operate; but it was enough. On April 11, just before dawn, Abu-Zaiad received a phone call. He answered, his voice groggy and annoyed. His presence confirmed, the line went dead. A Caesarea assassin pushed a button on a remote control, ripping the PLO terrorist to shreds. Mission accomplished.

Two months later, on June 13, 1973, a deafening explosion ripped through a Mercedes in Rome's city center. The two men in the car carried passports in the names of Abed Al-Hamid Shibi and Abed Al-Hadi Naka'a. Both died from their wounds not long after the explosion. The ambush, laid by Caesarea combatants, prevented a planned attack on the El Al offices in Rome, which were located opposite the parked car. The Mossad had stopped another attack dead in its tracks.

Days later, in late June 1973, Aharon Yariv announced that he was retiring from his post as advisor to the prime minister on terrorism. In a parting interview with the Israeli newspaper *Yediot Aharonot,* he spoke at length about Palestinian international terrorism. "Since the Sabena hijacking Palestinian groups have attempted sixty-seven attacks abroad that we know of; forty-eight of them failed or were prevented. It is quite possible there were additional attacks in the works that we know nothing about. I would like to point out that of the sixty-seven planned attacks, forty-eight were aimed at Israeli targets, and thirty-seven of those failed."

After nine months as the prime minister's advisor, the retired general decided to turn to politics. In hindsight, his retirement marked a transition, from an obsessive chase for terrorists and revenge to a routine war against Palestinian terrorism.

The assassinations in Europe and the Middle East, along with the astonishingly successful raid in Beirut, a Mossad-IDF collaboration, were starting to reap dividends. The mood in the agency lifted. There were clear signs of a lull in terror activity. The Mossad still buzzed with activity. Its expanded Caesarea unit was up to its eyeballs in work. Military Intelligence's Branch 4, already through with its technological overhaul, began introducing commandos into its ranks. These men, who, as Ehud Barak once said, "had seen the whites of the enemies' eyes," brought their knowledge of the field into the office. The Shabak, instructed by the Kopel Report to assume responsibility for the security and safety of Israel's embassies and consulates abroad, worked around the clock. A written code of security laws for the protection of Israelis abroad was enacted. From that moment forth, for instance, any official Israeli delegation, whether it be for sports, agriculture, or culture, would be accompanied by guards, armed if the host country permitted it.

Nine long months had passed since the Munich Massacre. Nine months of kinetic Israeli existence, the highs and lows, on the backdrop of perpetual chaos. The fervor to avenge the death of the athletes began to subside. A thirst for preventive and deterrent assassinations was replacing it. Many of the organization heads and PLO activists who were being targeted now had no connection to Munich or Fatah–Black September. Intelligence agency bosses feared another unexpected attack. That fear was what kept them awake at night. Shabak officers called Branch 4 at all hours, looking for fact-based warnings. Attacks had been prevented and were doubtless being deterred, but for years after Munich, terror attacks in Israel and abroad would continue nonetheless, and always took the intelligence agencies by complete surprise. "Come to the control room . . ." was still the first many officers would hear about an attack.

• • •

In his farewell interview, Yariv addressed the aspect of international collaboration in the war on terrorism. "The cooperation between Israel and other governments is an important factor in our fight. Not all contribute equally. In many cases we would like to see certain governments do far more in the fight against Arab terrorism. I am particularly irked by the forgiveness exhibited by some nations toward terrorists caught in the act. They are neither tried nor punished. In the long term, these nations will be burnt by this policy. In today's atmosphere it is simply naive to think that clemency and forgiveness toward Arab terrorism will reduce the risk of terror at home. On the contrary, firm steps against Arab terrorism will deter future terror within these nations."

Yariv bemoaned the intolerable ease with which weapons and explosives crossed European borders, even after the Munich Massacre. One foiled attempt took place on October 23, 1972, when a Palestinian in transit at Amsterdam's Schiphol Airport was stopped with forty pounds of explosives, twenty-one letter bombs, and a stash of grenades, detonators, and pistols. The contraband was "voluntarily" surrendered by the traveler, Kamal Al-Khatib, a Jerusalem-born Fatah activist, who was carrying an Algerian diplomatic passport. He was released several hours later and allowed to continue on his way. The authorization to free the man came from the top levels of the Dutch government, eliciting scathing criticism from the opposition parties in the Dutch parliament. Security officials at the airport were perplexed by the decision. Al-Khatib's mission began in Damascus and was to end in either Argentina or Brazil but, according to the senior-level security officials at the airport, he was prepared to leave the explosives in Amsterdam "for further care." Moreover, they said, his diplomatic immunity was useless to him as a defense, since he was not a diplomat serving in Holland, where immunity would have shielded him from local law.

The man's Algerian passport was the tip of an iceberg. In the late 1960s and early 1970s Algeria was an ardent and outspoken backer of Palestinian terror. In 1969, for example, the oil pipeline in the Golan Heights was blown up; only Algeria publicly supported the attack. Algeria alone supported the 1970 PFLP hijacking and exploding of five planes in Jordan, and it was again Algeria that registered a formal complaint against Switzerland at the U.N. when that nation decided to bring the attackers of an El Al plane in Zurich to trial. Israeli intelligence agencies had been claiming for years that Algerian embassies and consulates across Europe served as weapons caches and points of departure for Palestinian terrorists working under the guise of diplomats. Algerian embassies were buffet-style banquets for terrorists: all they had to do was walk through the door and help themselves.

Since the military coup that brought Colonel Muammar Qaddafi to power in late 1969, Libya had also aided and abetted terrorists with logistical support, weapons, shelter, and intelligence information, Israel would claim for years. The heads of state of other nations, such as Yemen, Syria, and Iraq, even publicly supported the hijacking of planes. The latter two went so far as to create and support Palestinian terror organizations that acted against Israel both within and beyond its territorial boundaries.

The Netherlands, like many other European countries, refused to take firm action against Palestinian terrorists, at a time when Europe was their main theater of operations. Many of the attacks were extortionate, demanding the release of certain prisoners in exchange for the resolution of a current standoff. A conciliatory tone was predominant. Abu-Iyad himself said that after Fatah terrorists opened fire on the Jordanian ambassador to Britain in downtown London, "The British authorities, like many of their European counterparts, preferred to avoid complications, taking no great pains to capture the Palestinian commandos."

Intelligence information was regularly passed from Israel to Europe to help prevent terror attacks. Suspects were apprehended before committing crimes but then released posthaste. If actually tried and convicted, terrorists frequently had their sentences commuted. A survey conducted by the Israeli Foreign Ministry found that 204 terrorists were convicted of terror-related felonies in countries outside the Middle East between 1968 and 1975; by late 1975, only three remained behind bars.

Leniency and forgiveness were the hallmark of many European intelligence agencies. Although Western European nations were on guard after the Munich Massacre, many reached secret agreements with the PLO. France, Italy, and West Germany all bargained for their safety, but the agreements did not always hold. Renegade Palestinian resistance groups refused the PLO's directives, acting where they pleased. "Munich illuminated a number of issues to the Americans, Germans, and others, but changed none of their axioms and beliefs," Lieutenant Colonel Jonathan Mor told me. "I traveled abroad, met European and American intelligence officers and tried to explain our thesis about international terrorism. They did not want to understand. For the Germans, French, and Americans it was a hard thing to swallow. They saw it as something light-years away from them. They usually looked at me with a face that said, 'What the hell is he talking about?' "

Israel continued to act alone in its efforts to prevent terror attacks, abiding by the ancient Hebrew adage: "If I am not for myself, then who will be for me? And if I am only for myself, what am I? And if not now, when?"

28 BOUDIA

Muhammad Boudia was a terrorism entrepreneur, a true professional in his trade, willing to contract his services to multiple Palestinian terror organizations. Throughout the summer of 1972, Boudia lived in Paris, in constant fear that he was next on the Mossad's hit list. He was right.

Boudia changed his daily routine regularly and took safety precautions. As the manager of a small theater, he was skilled in the arts of makeup and costume. The attractive thirty-six-year-old Algerian would spend the night with a woman and then leave her apartment in the morning dressed as an old man or a woman, in an attempt to shake any surveillance team that might be following him. Boudia did in fact evade the Caesarea surveillance units on numerous occasions, slipping into the Parisian crowds and disappearing. But every man has a weak point that will ultimately give him away. In Mossad terminology, this is referred to as the "Capture Point." Muhammad Boudia's Capture Point was his car. The elusive, wary terrorist inexplicably always drove the same gray Renault 16 with Parisian license plates, registered in

his name. This habit was a colossal security oversight that Caesarea would exploit.

Boudia always inspected his Renault before entering. He
checked the chassis for explosive devices and hand grenades before unlocking the car. Caesarea's agents took note. On the night
of Thursday, June 28, 1973, while he slept at the flat of one of his
girlfriends, they broke into Boudia's Renault, placing a lethal explosive device beneath the driver's seat. The Renault was parked
on Rue des Fossés Saint-Bernard next to the Faculty of Sciences
building in the Latin Quarter of Paris. Late the next morning,
Boudia returned to the car. An eyewitness described the event: "A
man in a gray suit arrived and got into the car. He started the engine. His feet were still on the pavement and he was immediately
swallowed by a ball of fire." An undercover Caesarea combatant
detonated the bomb by remote control, after verifying that there
were no innocent bystanders and that the man who got into the
car was, in fact, the target, Muhammad Boudia. Within minutes
of the explosion the police and fire departments arrived on the
scene. Firemen extinguished the blaze engulfing the car and collected Boudia's remains—the force of the blast splattered his
body parts over the cars parked nearby. "The explosive device
was large but the blast was concentrated in the center of the car,
preventing pedestrians from being injured," determined the investigating police officer. The victim was quickly identified. "We
knew the man well. He's been on file," the investigating officer
commented dryly.

Boudia was a left-wing intellectual and an amateur actor. He
fought with the underground National Front for the Liberation
of Algeria (FLN in its French acronym) against the French occupation in Algeria. The demolition expert's role in subversive terror attacks on French soil aimed at the oil reserves earned him

about three years in a French jail. When Algeria gained independence in 1962, he was released. He returned to Algeria, to live in the capital city of Algiers, and was appointed manager of the national theater by the first Algerian president, Ahmed Ben Bella, his close friend. Three years later, Houari Boumédienne, the opposition leader, rose to power in Algeria. Boudia fled, settling in France. In Paris, he continued to work in his primary field of interest—theater. He was appointed manager of the small avantgarde Théâtre de l'Ouest (Theater of the West). The energetic artist worked long hours, but still managed to find time during his short life to party, to marry and to divorce three times, and to conduct endless love affairs.

Women loved him. That was evident during Eveline Barge's testimony at her trial in the military court in Lod, Israel, in the summer of 1971. She had been recruited by Boudia, and her testimony provided a keyhole view into his scandalous world. Barge, twenty-six, an English teacher by trade, was a stunning Frenchwoman who started working as a part-time cashier at the theater and promptly became Boudia's mistress. During her defense she told the judges that she had fallen for his charisma and charm, had internalized and adopted his leftist political beliefs, and was sent by him to carry out a terror attack in Tel Aviv. In her testimony, she also confessed to having assisted in the detonation of a Gulf Oil facility in the Netherlands port of Rotterdam in the spring of 1971.

It was becoming clear to Mossad agents that Boudia was a wizard at recruiting people for his deadly plots. Most were women: Eveline Barge, sentenced to fourteen years in prison, motivated by love; Nadia and Marlene Bradley, daughters of a Moroccan businessman, sent to Israel at his behest with fake passports and powerful explosives, motivated by a thirst for adventure and the forbidden; Pierre and Edith Borghalter, an elderly French couple, motivated, perhaps, by the 3,500 francs they received in exchange for their services. Boudia sent Barge, the Bradley sisters, and the elderly couple to Israel as part of his grandiose plan to orchestrate coordinated explosions in nine Tel Aviv hotels over the Passover holiday. They were intercepted and arrested by Shabak. Had it been successful, the attack would have killed many innocent tourists and Israelis.

Boudia collaborated with the PFLP in the planning of the foiled Passover attack. Two operations against oil facilities, the one in Rotterdam in the middle of March 1971, and the other, in Trieste, Italy, at the start of August 1972, were designed and executed by Boudia and his new close friend Ali Hassan Salameh.

Firemen in Trieste prevented a major disaster by extinguishing the fire before it could ignite an outsized fuel tank. Black September took responsibility for the attack, publishing a formal announcement in Beirut. During the Italian police's investigation, Boudia's name came up. Based on the testimonies of detainees suspected of involvement, the police issued a warrant for his arrest in 1973. (After his death, it surfaced that Boudia was wanted for questioning by Interpol, as well as the Swiss and Dutch police.)

The Mossad realized that the connection between Boudia and Salameh was growing stronger, that Boudia, who often worked for the PFLP, wholeheartedly extended his services to Salameh and Fatah. There is no doubt that the cooperation between Boudia and Fatah, operating under the name Black September, was first and foremost the result of the special personal connection he forged with Salameh. The two had met in Europe, loved the good life, and became fast friends. Their friendship ripened, leading to the terror attacks carried out in Europe. Ali Hassan Salameh supplied the logistical services and infrastructure for the attacks; Boudia executed the missions. The Mossad received a steady flow of information indicating that Boudia and Salameh were plotting a high-profile terror attack against Israeli targets in Europe.

Muhammad Boudia was not remotely involved in the Munich Massacre. The Mossad did not try to make a false connection this time. Boudia's dark past—the thwarted attack in Israel, the successful attacks carried out in Rotterdam and Trieste, and the near-certainty about future terror plans were sufficiently incriminating. The French investigating officer assigned to the assassination announced in front of a French reporter, "He was an active terrorist who was wanted for his role in the explosion of the oil terminal in Trieste, Italy."

On Sunday, July 1, 1973, R., Caesarea's chief intelligence officer, arrived very early at his cramped office in the Hadar Dafna Building in Tel Aviv. He went straight to the locked cabinet, turned the key, and drew a large black X over the photo of Boudia's face. The target of Caesarea's assassination operations had been executed.

Caesarea's combatants and staff officers at Tel Aviv headquarters earned many pats on the back. "You do holy work," they heard often. Harari's combatants called him Caesar behind his back. He was flattered; he knew that his people would follow him through hell and high water. But their success was going to their heads, a dangerous overconfidence that would lead to tragedy.

In the Mossad's weekly meeting of division and unit commander heads, Zvi Zamir praised Harari, in front of the full forum, on the smooth and perfect operation that had left no Israeli traces in the field. Harari just sat in his seat and smiled. He and his group's endless investment were yielding results that far surpassed expectations. Harari did not pause for a second. His men continued to follow his lead and search for trails leading to the next man on the assassination list. Time was not on their side— every passing day gave the enemy the opportunity to devise new plans that the Israelis would have to thwart. On the Mossad's hit list, one name stood out among the top five. Ali Hassan Salameh.

29 THE BLUNDER IN LILLEHAMMER

At the municipal pool in Lillehammer, a peaceful vacation town in Norway, children were splashing and making noise in the heated water while a dozen adult swimmers did their laps up and down the length of the pool, maintaining a steady pace. A young, Middle Eastern–looking man in his thirties stood in the shallow water talking with a bearded European man of similar age. The two did not notice when Marianne Gladnikoff entered the water in her no-frills one-piece blue bathing suit and started to swim. Gladnikoff maneuvered herself closer to the two men as she swam, glancing at the dark man's face. Each time she swam past, she had a few seconds to examine him. She noticed that the two were speaking in French but the children's noise prevented her from making out their words. Marianne was the youngest member of the Caesarea surveillance team that was rushed to Lillehammer, one hundred miles north of Oslo, Norway's capital, to close in on the "bastard," whose extensive travels had brought him to the sleepy town.

The man with the Middle Eastern appearance was thought to be Ali Hassan Salameh, head of Fatah's Force 17 and a member of Arafat's inner circle. According to Israeli intelligence, he was one of the leaders of Black September and had been involved in the planning of the attack at the Munich Olympics. Mike Harari and his officers assumed that Salameh was using the pool as a safe meeting point, where conversation would be inconspicuous and could not be overheard. The European man, they figured, was most likely a *saya'an* involved in an operational plan to carry out another major terror attack against Israeli targets, this time in Scandinavia.

After weeks and months, thousands of hours of reconnaissance, frustrating waiting and watching, Salameh's trail had finally been picked up by Caesarea's assassination squad. In a few hours they would be sending him into the next world. The operational and intelligence achievement this assassination represented would be immense, more significant even than the Spring of Youth. Some whispered that success in Lillehammer would take Mike Harari, the rising star, a significant step closer to the Mossad's top spot.

The hunt for Salameh had stretched across Western Europe since the Munich Massacre. In the summer of 1973, Israeli intelligence received information that he was near the city of Ulm, in West Germany; then they got word that he had moved to Lille, in France; then back to West Germany. Next, he went north to Hamburg, on the shores of the Elbe River, where the trail went cold.

At the same time, Mossad HQ received very general intelligence regarding Fatah's intention to perpetrate a terrorist attack against Israeli targets in Scandinavia, most likely at the Israeli embassy in Sweden. This intelligence flowed in just as Salameh headed north to Hamburg. With all clues pointing north, intelligence shifted its focus to Stockholm, Sweden's capital.

On July 14, 1973, Israeli intelligence learned that a mysterious young Algerian living in Geneva, Switzerland, flew to Copenhagen, Denmark, on short notice. The Mossad suspected the man, Kamal Benaman, of serving as a European liaison for Black September. Benaman, twenty-eight, a dark, handsome Algerian, had left Geneva for a meeting with the boss, Ali Hassan Salameh. According to Mossad HQ estimates, Salameh was to meet with Benaman to finalize the details of Black September's terror operation in Scandinavia, one that Salameh would command. Benaman was spotted at the Copenhagen airport as he boarded an Oslo-bound plane. Then he disappeared.

A large Mossad team, totaling about a dozen men and women, was hastily organized and flown to Oslo. Their mission was to locate the two men who were set to rendezvous—Benaman and Salameh. On July 18, after an exhaustive four-day hunt, the trackers learned that Benaman had already left Oslo for the northern town of Lillehammer. The surveillance crew, led by staff officer Avraham Gemer, followed him. Despite the unforeseen location, the Mossad's estimate remained the same—Benaman and Salameh would still meet, most likely in Lillehammer.

Israeli intelligence gathering was incessant and earnest, but the intelligence itself was often of medium to poor quality and incomplete. Low-level sources supplied secondhand information. The Tzomet division, charged with running agents, was still struggling to gain adequate intelligence. A year had passed since Sabena, Munich was ten months old, and when it came to the key players Tzomet was still searching in the dark. Numerous case officers, scattered throughout Europe, invested endless hours recruiting quality sources. Despite their hard work and complete motivation, Tzomet was not getting enough reliable information from its agents. It received virtually no solid intelligence about planned terror attacks and far too little information of the sort that could help in the planning of assassination operations.

For twenty-four hours, the Mossad team could find no trace of Salameh in Lillehammer. Surveillance crews in four cars circled the city, searching the streets, coffee shops, and hotel lobbies, to no avail. On Friday afternoon, July 20, Benaman, who was being trailed at all times, sat on the balcony of the Karoline Café, near Lillehammer Town Hall. Two Middle Eastern–looking men approached him and sat down at his table. The three talked for about an hour. To a member of the surveillance team, one of the men looked like Ali Hassan Salameh.

Harari and Avraham Gemer were jubilant. "We got him!" The suspect left the café on a bicycle a short while later. The surveillance crews zeroed in.

By the next day, Harari and Gemer were increasingly certain of the terrorist's identity. As they set about sculpting an operational plan for his assassination, Marianne Gladnikoff was sent into the waters of the municipal pool while the surveillance crews waited outside.

Ali Hassan Salameh was a central target for intelligence collection; any agent working for the Mossad was asked and pressured for information about the elusive terrorist. But despite his high profile, operative intelligence regarding Salameh was scant, incomplete, secondhand, and in many cases arrived only after the fact: "Salameh was here . . ." or "Salameh visited there . . ." were phrases Mossad *katsas* heard all too often. The decision to crown the man in the café as Ali Hassan Salameh was made on the basis of very slim intelligence. The available information was certainly insufficient to authorize an assassination. But all this can only be said in retrospect. At the time, the field operatives were certain that Ali Hassan Salameh had met with Kamal Benaman at the Karoline Café. They had tracked the mysterious Benaman from Geneva to the remote town of Lillehammer. The same man who met with Benaman spoke French at his next meeting in the municipal pool—a language the Mossad believed Salameh spoke well. And when the man in Lillehammer was matched up with a picture of Salameh, the final piece of the puzzle snapped into place: the images bore a remarkable resemblance.

The surveillance squads followed Salameh as he left the municipal pool and entered Bragsang, a store with a coffee shop. At noon, he exited the shop accompanied by a young Norwegian-looking woman. She had light blond hair and was clearly pregnant. The two got on a local bus, a surveillance car following. The couple got off at the bus stop in Nivo, a residential neighborhood in the western part of town, and stepped into one of the new apartment buildings at Rugdeveien 2A. The commander of the mission, Avraham Gemer, instructed his team to station four cars and five surveillance posts around the building, to cover all exit and entry points. Gemer did not intend to let the prey escape this time. The surveillance team took walkie-talkies, were told to stay alert and to blend in with their surroundings.

Meanwhile, two undercover combatants arrived separately at the Opland Turis Hotel in the town. The assassins waited for a call from Harari. The Mossad combatants were dark-skinned, had black hair, and drove rental cars with Oslo plates. An anomalous sight in this sleepy town, they attracted attention.

In the evening hours, the man fingered as Salameh and his pregnant partner left the apartment for the local movie theater.

The Israeli surveillance crew had no trouble following; the woman wore a bright yellow raincoat. The couple did not act tense or anxious. They did not try to shake the surveillance. They went straight to the box office in Lillehammer's only movie theater and bought a pair of tickets for *Where Eagles Dare,* an American war movie starring Clint Eastwood and Richard Burton. It chronicled a group of American soldiers on a suicide mission at the end of World War II. An excited and keyed-up member of the surveillance squad called the rest of the crew, who were in the middle of dinner, to tell them to get ready. The squad spread out to their designated spots, coiled and waiting.

No one on the surveillance squad questioned certain incongruities. Why was Ali Hassan Salameh, the notorious Palestinian terrorist, who was known to be living in Beirut, riding a bicycle in remote Lillehammer, Norway—population: twenty thousand? Why was he so familiar with the streets? Why did he take a pregnant blond Norwegian to the movies? Salameh, despite his reputation at the Mossad and Israeli intelligence as a serial playboy, was married and had two young sons. It required a giant leap to assume that Salameh was leading a double life with a pregnant Norwegian. No one was sent to check his apartment, to look for drafts of terrorist plots. Harari and his agents believed that they had found their man, even if it required a pernicious suspension of logic and several cut corners.

Zvi Zamir was on his way to Lillehammer, flying on a fake passport, undercover. As in previous assassination operations, he asked to be near the operation and to authorize it from up close. But by late evening he was stuck at Schiphol Airport, waiting for a connecting flight to Oslo.

"Is this our man?" Zamir asked, after the operators connected him.

"Yes," Harari answered.

"Are you sure?" added Zamir.

"Yes," responded Harari.

"Okay, you have my authorization."

That was the second conversation between Harari and Zamir that day. The first time they spoke, Zamir requested that Harari verify, as he would again, that they had found the man they sought.

At 2235 hours the couple left the movie theater and walked in silence to the bus stop. Harari sent the two assassins to Porobakakan Street, where they waited in darkness next to one of the houses. The bus arrived at the stop and the couple boarded without hesitation. The surveillance team followed. The couple got off the bus, calm and relaxed. They held hands, talking quietly to each other as they strolled along Porobakakan Street, walking leisurely up the inclining street toward their house. A car coming in the opposite direction stopped several yards away. The two men in the backseat jumped out, withdrew their silenced Berettas, and shot the man ten times at close range. They stepped back into the car and sped off down the hill.

The bullets had torn through the man's vital organs. The woman knelt down next to him, screaming wildly. A neighbor, a young nurse named Dagny Bring, looked out of her window and called the police. Within three minutes, a police car arrived. Ten minutes later, an ambulance arrived; attempts at resuscitation failed. Fifteen minutes after arriving at the local hospital, the man was pronounced dead.

According to the original plan, Harari and the two assassins were to leave Lillehammer separately, then travel south to Oslo as fast as possible; by the early morning hours they would be scattered in different countries throughout Europe. The members of the surveillance team also headed for Oslo. There, they were supposed to return the rental cars, turn over the keys to the rented apartments they had used during the operation, and sweep, making sure that no "tails" or footprints had been left behind. They were to wait a few days and then get out of Oslo.

Early in the morning, R., Caesarea's chief intelligence officer, called his colleague in Branch 4, a talented young captain from the Targets section, and revealed, "We took him out. We got Salameh, in Norway."

"What? That's impossible!"

"I'm telling you, we got him," R. insisted.

"But it can't be," the officer shouted, slamming his fist down hard on the desk. "He wasn't there. It's a mistake!"

When the head of Branch 4 debriefed his officers about the amazing assassination in Norway, the officers, appalled, said, "It can't be, he wasn't there."

In Monday's Norwegian newspapers, giant headlines announced the murder of a young Moroccan by the name of Achmed Bouchiki, killed in Lillehammer on Saturday night. Caesarea officers suspected that the name was just another one of the cover identities Ali Hassan Salameh used while traveling abroad. But they were terribly wrong; they had made an awful mistake. Caesarea's assassination team had trailed and murdered the wrong man.

A reporter and photographer had rushed to the scene right after the murder. Interviews with eyewitnesses and neighbors revealed the presence of strangers in fancy cars, Mercedes and Mazdas, driving around the neighborhood, pausing in front of the apartment building earlier that day. The reporter knew he had a major story: this was the first murder in Lillehammer in forty years. He had no idea what he really had.

The reporter knew Bouchiki from around town. In a two-page article he described the man as a thirty-year-old Moroccan who had lived in Lillehammer for the past four years. His wife, Toril Larsen Bouchiki, was Norwegian. She was in her seventh month of pregnancy. Bouchiki, the article noted, had emigrated from Morocco in the hope of improving his life. He worked as a waiter, and supplemented his salary with a part-time job at the local pool. Years later it became clear that the meeting with Kamal Benaman on the balcony of the Karoline Café was an innocent get-together between two North Africans, a chance to speak a few words of Arabic and catch up on news from home.

Oslo papers raised the possibility of a connection between the arraignment of four foreigners with foreign passports—Patricia Roxburgh, Leslie Orbaum, Marianne Gladnikoff, and Dan Art—and the shooting in Lillehammer. The initial reports were unclear, unable to explain how the four detainees were connected to the murdered man. Some raised the possibility that it was a drug deal gone wrong.

On Sunday morning, Dan Art, an Israeli of Danish origin who went by the name Dan Arbel in Israel, was taken into custody. He was using his real passport while fulfilling an auxiliary role in the Mossad mission. He was recruited for this mission at the last minute, brought on board because of his command of the language, a skill the Caesarea combatants lacked. He could read the street signs, verify addresses over the telephone, order hotel rooms, rent cars, and find suitable safe houses. Marianne Glad-nikoff, a Swedish Jew who had been picked by Caesarea's human resources division shortly after she moved to Israel—and had been suggested as a suitable candidate for support and logistical operations in Scandinavian countries—was arrested along with Art/Arbel. The two were stopped at the Pornavo Airport returning the team's rental cars. They had no cover story prepared and failed to explain why they were driving cars with plates the police were looking for (the two cars had been spotted at a roadblock speeding out of Lillehammer—and struck an officer as suspicious). Neither of the two was a Mossad combatant. They talked as soon as they were taken in for questioning. The information they provided led to the arrest of two senior members of the surveillance unit. The veteran agents were traveling undercover as British citizen Leslie Orbaum and Canadian citizen Patricia Roxburgh.

Leslie Orbaum was none other than Avraham Gemer, staff officer and head of the unit. He was a tough and stubborn man who did not cooperate with the investigators and stuck to his hole-ridden cover story, that he was British citizen Orbaum, aged twenty-nine, a teacher and librarian from Leeds, vacationing in Norway.

"Your name can't be Leslie Orbaum," the police investigator charged. "This man doesn't exist. We checked thoroughly."

"So I don't have a name," Gemer answered angrily.

Patricia Roxburgh, the woman taken into custody, was actually Sylvia Rafael. She was a Caesarea combatant who had participated in numerous operations in Europe, Lebanon, Syria, and Egypt. An attractive thirty-six-year-old Jew, Rafael was born in Capetown, South Africa. She was an amateur photographer. In 1963, she arrived in Israel; by 1965, she had been recruited by Caesarea's human resources department. Her skills as a combatant were evident from the start. She was calm, quick-witted, and trustworthy. She was the type of woman who could mingle in any society and engender a feeling of security and trust. Rafael preferred to keep her independence, though: she did not join the Mossad full-time, choosing to participate only in certain missions. Caesarea kept her close at hand and requested her services often. Her hobby had served her well on numerous occasions. Using a Canadian or South African passport, she presented herself as a freelance reporter and photographer scouring the area for a juicy story.

Rafael claimed to be a Canadian freelance journalist on vacation who happened to meet Leslie Orbaum, an old acquaintance, by chance, at the Zurich airport. On the spot the two decided to travel to Norway for a vacation. There they met Art/Arbel and Gladnikoff and decided to share an apartment with them.

The investigators were not convinced. There were serious contradictions in the four versions of events the detainees recounted. They could not corroborate the details of the time they lived together.

When the Oslo police searched Dan Art's belongings they found documents with a phone number that led to the arrest of two additional Israelis, Zvi Steinberg and Michael Dorf, who were staying in the private residence of Yigal Eyal, security officer for the Israeli embassy in Oslo. The two men were logistics and communications agents for the Mossad. They had found temporary shelter in the security officer's apartment. In Steinberg's coat pocket, the police found a first-class train ticket from Oslo to Copenhagen, set to leave at 2210 hours that night. As they searched through Steinberg's and Dorf's suitcases and personal items, more incriminating evidence was discovered. The Caesarea agents had been negligent during the final stages of the operation.

With Dorf and Steinberg arrested, the number of detained Israelis rose to six.

Caesarea's grand pretensions were unveiled during the investigation of the shaky Dan Art/Arbel, a claustrophobic, and Marianne Gladnikoff, the junior agent. Blindly determined, the Mossad had arrived in drowsy Lillehammer and assassinated a man whom they mistakenly took for a Palestinian terrorist. The police investigation and the detainees' testimonies revealed the incompetent, unprofessional behavior of many team members. Caesarea's senior officers had a raging desire to complete the mission at any cost, which caused them to act without even a minimal amount of caution. They were arrogant, reckless, overconfident, and stubborn. Their fundamental mind-set flaws were the main reason the wrong man died and the mission was exposed. Mike Harari and the two assassins managed to escape by the skin of their teeth. Only by chance did they avoid being caught.

The Israeli government was unsure how to handle the arrest of the six Mossad operatives in Norway. One of Golda Meir's worst nightmares had come true. There were long conversations about the right way to respond. The basic question: should Israel take responsibility for the assassination or try to distance itself? As in the past (in several incidents in Arab countries), the government in Jerusalem chose to take the middle path. Without publicly acknowledging their role in sending the team, the government sent Foreign Ministry legal advisor Meir Rosenne to Norway, and shortly thereafter, Eleazar Palmor, a Foreign Ministry official who was appointed special advisor to the embassy. The government ordered Palmor to follow the trial closely, establish connections with local legal bodies, and tend to the needs of the detainees.

In Golda Meir's office in Jerusalem, Zvi Zamir and Mike

Harari turned in their resignations in the presence of her military aide, Yisrael Lior. She refused to accept them. "There are people in jail," she said. "You can't get up and leave; there is work to be done."

On Friday, four days after the episode was exposed, Meir sent Lior to Mossad headquarters in Tel Aviv, to check on Harari's emotional and mental state. Harari did not blame himself for the mistake or the detention of six agents under his command. When asked about the embarrassing affair, he said, with an almost Clintonian eloquence, "I take responsibility upon myself, but not the guilt." At other times, he said, "When the sharpest combatants succeeded, it was my success; when they failed, it was my failure."

The six sat for a public trial, the focus of intense media coverage in Norway, Israel, and the rest of the world. Sylvia Rafael impressed reporters with her calm appearance and witty demeanor. When Avraham Gemer was called to the witness stand, he sat there a short while, stubborn and distracted. Only Dan Art/Arbel appeared shocked and afraid. He wrung his hands nervously as he explained his reasons for joining the "Scandinavian mission." He said that the operation appealed to him because his expenses were paid and he had just purchased a new house in Israel, which he wanted to furnish. Asked the prosecutor: "Did you really believe that Israel would step in to assist an illegal group working in Norway?" Answered Art/Arbel: "To tell you the truth, because of the good relations between Norway and Israel, I thought that the issue would be solved in private between the two nations. It was my innocence that made me think like that." Arbel said on the stand that he had given the Oslo police investigators a number in the Hadar Dafna Building in Tel Aviv—256-230—so that they could confirm his story.

Avraham Gemer was incensed. Sensitive intelligence was being bandied about in public. He requested, by way of his representative, that the trial resume behind closed doors. The court agreed. Meanwhile, the reporters dashed out of the courtroom and ordered the operator to connect them to 256-230 in Tel Aviv. A recording with a message in English said, "This number is no longer connected."

On February 1, 1974, the six were sentenced. Michael Dorf, a communications and codes agent, was the only one found not guilty and released. The five other Israelis were found guilty and sentenced as follows: Zvi Steinberg, logistical agent for the operation, was sentenced to one year in prison for gathering information for a foreign country; Marianne Gladnikoff was sentenced to two and half years for her involvement in the murder. Dan Art/Arbel was sentenced to five years for having secondhand knowledge of a premeditated murder. Avraham Gemer and Sylvia Rafael were sentenced to five and a half years for their involvement in the murder. The court found that all six played minor roles in the shooting of Bouchiki, when compared to the assassins and the operational planners who had managed to escape.

The bitter mistake that cost the waiter, Achmed Bouchiki, his life, weighed like a millstone on the shoulders of the state of Israel. It had long-lasting effects on Israel—in its relations with Norway and with other nations, as it was suddenly seen as a state carrying out its own brand of international terror.

For years, Israel denied responsibility for the incident. Only in January 1996 did Prime Minister Shimon Peres veer away from years of Israeli government policy. He sent a leading Israeli lawyer to Oslo to conduct compensation negotiations with the family of the murdered victim. Israel agreed to pay for the shooting of the father of the family without taking official responsibility for the act. The negotiations continued for but a few hours. An agreement was quickly reached, in which Israel expressed regret over the actions in Lillehammer and offered compensation to the family totaling almost $400,000.

Thirty-one years after the court's verdict, on a warm, clear winter day, veteran Caesarea combatants and staff officers attended the funeral of their friend, combatant Sylvia Rafael, who had lived for the past twenty years in South Africa with her partner, Norwegian lawyer Anneus Schodt, her defense attorney during the Oslo trial. During the long legal ordeal, they had fallen in love. He had left his family following her release from prison. On the afternoon of February 15, 2005, she was buried in the small cemetery at Kibbutz Ramat Ha'Kovesh, which had adopted her during her incarceration. She was buried at age sixty-seven, in the heart of the fields and in the shade of cypress trees.

Dozens of friends, many of them with salt-and-pepper hair and walking sticks, stood around her grave. Three former heads of the Mossad came to pay their final respects. They stood around the grave. Mike Harari, Caesarea commander, the man responsible for the Lillehammer mission that landed her in jail, offered a eulogy: "Sylvia was a Caesarean of noble stock, who volunteered to be a combatant for the nation of Israel. . . . They say that those who don't act, don't make mistakes, and never have problems. We acted! We did so much and we succeeded. When we succeeded, they called us 'professionals,' 'the hand of God,' and more. And when we failed, they called us '*shlomeils*.' The truth is we weren't *shlomeils*, and we weren't professionals. We simply fulfilled our mission to defend the nation of Israel."

30 CLOUDY SKIES SAVE ARAFAT

Lieutenant Colonel Jonathan Mor picked up the scrambled phone. "Mor," he said, tight for time, preoccupied by the dozens of raw intelligence reports that had landed on his desk since early morning. The person on the other end of the line was equally direct. "Initial, unchecked reports show that Arafat is at Fatah headquarters in Nabatiya, for a meeting with local commanders. We'll be back in touch as necessary."

Mor swallowed, no longer distracted by paperwork. "You sure it's him?"

"That's what it sounds like," was the reply.

"Keep me updated," Mor said before slamming down the phone. He pondered the news for two beats, then called the deputy commander of Military Intelligence. He relayed the facts as he had heard them.

"Come upstairs," the colonel said.

The opportunity that had presented itself was clear to both of them—Yasser Arafat, chairman of the PLO and commander of

Fatah, a man high on Israel's hit list for years, was in south Lebanon, a few minutes' flight time from Israel's northern border. Mor walked into the colonel's office and presented the facts: ten minutes ago Arafat seemed to have entered Fatah's forward command center in Nabatiya, south Lebanon, five miles north of Israel's border. There was no positive ID of the man. The only way they could be sure was to have a look at the parking lot of the house that served as their HQ—if it was lined with Mercedes-Benz cars and top-of-the-line Jeeps, they would know. A visit from Arafat would draw all of the area's commanders. He did not visit the trenches that often; no one would miss the occasion.

Five minutes later, Mor and the colonel presented themselves outside the office of Chief of Staff David Elazar. They were escorted straight through. Elazar smiled when they entered. He knew both of them well. After a sixty-second presentation of the facts, the three of them left the office and walked through the door that led to the civilian half of the building, to the office of the defense minister. Although only thirty yards divided the two offices, the separation was kept stark and clear. Moshe Dayan listened to the news. "I'll pass this on to Golda. Get ready. And get me some verification." Before they turned from the room Dayan already had Golda on the phone. The conversation was over in seconds. He looked back at the uniformed men. "She authorized it. But she also demands verification that it's him."

The Chief of Staff sent Mor to "The Pit"—the air force control room dug several stories under the soft, sandy earth of the IDF headquarters. From there, Mor could supervise the mission. Moments later, an order was sent to the northern Ramat David airbase to arm a foursome of F-4 Phantoms with quarter-ton bombs. From the runway to Nabatiya was seven minutes flight time. A single-engine surveillance aircraft was already in the air, heading north. The pilot of the slow-flying Cessna had received orders from the office of the chief of staff before they went to Dayan's office. Each minute counted. The squadron's best aerial reconnaissance man sat behind the pilot, studying Nabatiya as it appeared on long strips of aerial photos. His mission was to locate the parking lot and answer one simple question—empty or full? He did not know that Arafat was suspected of being present.

Mor looked at his watch agitatedly. His feet were bouncing, his back sweating. "I'm overseeing one of the most important missions in the history of the country—the mission to eliminate Yasser Arafat," he thought to himself. Then he looked at the air force officer handling the mission from his end. He was all business, switching phones and radio receivers, issuing short and clear orders. It seemed to Mor that this officer and the other air force officers were too pressed for time to feel history in the making. After ten minutes of nerve-racking tension, the aerial reconnaissance man radioed, announcing calmly that he was over the borderline, five miles from the parking lot. "I have 8/8ths across the board," he said. Everyone in the pit realized the implications. In meteorological terms 8/8ths describes the fraction of the sky covered by opaque clouds: visibility was nil.

Leaning back in his chair, Mor let out a deep, remorseful sigh. The room around him was filled with the sound of the air force officers folding up the special mission. What a shame, he thought to himself. Yasser Arafat, leader of the PLO, owed his life to 8/8ths cloud cover.

Assassination missions had fallen low on the Mossad and Military Intelligence list of priorities. The were two reasons for this. The first was the failure in Lillehammer. The debacle that resulted in the death of an innocent man and sent six Mossad operatives to jail led to the immediate cessation of assassination missions.

The Mossad's image had been tarnished at home and abroad. It was one of the Mossad's toughest hours. Their confidence was shaken, their prestige tarnished.

Senior officers from within their ranks immediately began an in-house investigation. Caesarea and the Facha division, which supplied the initial faulty intelligence that led to the debacle, were called on to assist. The internal investigative committee prodded, poked, and probed. The report they handed in to Zvi Zamir detailed all aspects of the disastrous mission and the operational lessons to be learned from it.

But before the agency could learn any lessons a second blow was dealt: war. On October 6, 1973, Yom Kippur, the Jewish Day of Atonement, the Syrian and Egyptian armies coordinated a surprise invasion of Israeli-controlled territory on the Golan Heights and the Sinai Peninsula. The attack came under the guise of innocent border maneuvers. Israeli intelligence agencies had failed dismally in not seeing through the Egyptian-Syrian ruse.

There was a cessation of terror during the war, the Palestinian organizations waiting on the sidelines for the elimination of Israel. Military Intelligence's Branch 4 was shut, its officers dispersed to different units until the end of the war, which would claim over 2,500 Israeli lives.

The inability to predict the war was a colossal intelligence failure, a nine on the Richter scale. The Parliamentary Commission of Inquiry under the jurisdiction of Supreme Court Justice Shimon Agranat, which was set into motion to investigate the failure, kept the senior officers busy, as they exchanged accusations of culpability. Few senior officers escaped the fray. The committee's findings were grave. Major General Eli Zeira, commander of Military Intelligence, and Lieutenant General David Elazar, the IDF's Chief of Staff, were both forced to step down.

One of the few officers not involved in the squabble was Lieutenant Colonel Mor, who afterward did everything in his power to push for Mossad and IDF missions outside the country—like the one that fell into his lap when Arafat visited Nabatiya.

In September 1974 the top spot at the Mossad changed hands. Zvi Zamir, fifty-two, stepped down. Yitzhak Rabin, the new Prime Minister and former IDF Chief of Staff, a man untainted by the 1973 war, appointed his close friend Major General (ret.) Yitzhak Hofi. Hofi had shed his uniform two months earlier, after skillfully leading the Northern Command during the conflict. A cool-headed and conservative army man, he knew little of the Mossad's ways. He took to learning all he could, while addressing the recommendations of the Agranat Commission, including, among other things, starting an independent intelligence analysis wing. In 1976 the Facha division was formed as an independent unit, separate from Tzomet, housing all branches of operational intelligence analysis under one roof. Caesarea, under the guiding hand of Mike Harari, was reorganized. New departments and new branches in the chain of command were put into place. Kidon, a small, secretive assassination unit, was created. Caesarea was renamed several times, but the old name never wore off—it endures today as a nickname.

Hofi served as head of the Mossad for eight years, from 1974 to 1982. As opposed to his predecessor, he felt no obligation to avenge the Munich Massacre. As far as he was concerned the terrible shock of war, to both the defense establishment and the civilian population, did not allow for the type of single-minded focus necessary to hunt down the perpetrators of Munich to the end. Munich-based retribution was downgraded among the Mossad's priorities.

The primary mission for Hofi was rehabilitating and rebuilding the Mossad itself. Postwar reality demanded a shift in priorities. Manpower was diverted elsewhere. But terror attacks within

Israeli cities meant the Mossad had to be prepared to respond. Only one and a half years after taking the reins, the cautious Hofi hesitantly authorized preventive assassinations in Europe and the Middle East. At first, the Munich perpetrators were not targeted. But that would change.

31 OVERSEAS TERRORISM GRINDS TO A HALT

Dr. Wadi Haddad, the international man of terror responsible for dozens of airline hijackings and other earthshaking attacks against Israeli, American, and European targets the world over, died a slow, painful death in a grim East German hospital. The Palestinian doctor flew to Germany from Iraq, terminally ill. Once a fat man, he was now weak and emaciated, confined to his bed, waiting out his days. He died on March 30, 1978, only forty-eight years old.

The few dozen loyalists who had left the PFLP with Haddad were hard-pressed to explain the riddle of his torturous death. He died of an unknown terminal disease that attacked and debilitated his immune system. They could not be certain if his death was natural or induced. His more imaginative friends believed that Haddad's Iraqi patron, the ominous Vice President Saddam Hussein, had the doctor secretly poisoned once he was no longer useful to that regime. As always, some saw the hand of the Mossad in Haddad's death, claiming poisoning, but lacking any proof. Over the years the conspiracy theories dissipated and only the bitter fact of his inexplicable end remained. The bachelor, having amassed riches from years of terrorist activity, left millions of dollars to his sister.

For years Israel kept silent on the matter. Now it is possible to reveal that Dr. Haddad died an unnatural death. Poison was slipped into his food. The Mossad had sought to kill him ever since they learned that he was the mastermind behind hijackings carried out by the PFLP. They figured assassination was the only way to stop further deadly plans.

Haddad was a prolific and skilled terrorist. He was the first to hijack an El Al plane, on July 23, 1968. After weeks of captivity, Israel, headed at the time by Prime Minister Levi Eshkol, freed Palestinian prisoners in exchange for the hostages—the first and last time the Israeli government would ever bow to terrorist extortion. That El Al hijacking was the first in a series of plane hijackings designed to raise the profile of the Palestinian predicament. In September 1970, Dr. George Habash, the leader of the PFLP, the Marxist Palestinian terror organization that he founded along with Haddad, flew to North Korea on business. While he was away, Haddad had five planes hijacked. They were flown to Jordan, emptied, and then exploded for the cameras.

His operatives hijacked a Lufthansa flight en route from New Delhi, India, to Germany, forcing it to land in Aden, Yemen. Lufthansa paid several million dollars ransom for the plane and the passengers. Detractors of the supposedly Marxist terrorist claimed that Haddad deposited some $1 million in his own account. He was responsible for the PFLP's relationship with international terrorist organizations in Europe, Asia, and South America, offering them training facilities in Lebanon and strengthening their ties. One result: the Marxist Japanese Red Army attack at Lod Airport in 1972.

Haddad and his followers left the mainstream of the PFLP after that bold-headline attack, quarreling over the necessity of overseas terrorism. In October 1972 his men carried out the dubious Lufthansa hijacking that secured the freedom of the three surviving Munich terrorists. Determined to continue carrying out high-profile attacks outside Israel, his men were responsible for a December 21, 1975, attack on OPEC headquarters in Vienna and a late June 1976 hijacking of an Air France flight on its way from Israel.

Haddad was also willing to assist other terrorist organizations. In late February 1973, still living in Beirut, Haddad was asked by his good friend Abu-Iyad to falsify entry visas to Sudan, facilitating the attack on the embassy in Khartoum. Haddad created the visas in his print workshop within six hours.

Finally, on June 28, 1976, Haddad's men, with the assistance of the German Baader-Meinhof Gang, hijacked an Air France Airbus 747 en route from Israel to Paris, forcing the plane to land in Entebbe, Uganda. On July 4, 1976, the American Bicentennial, the hostage situation was resolved by a team of Israeli commandos led by Sayeret Matkal. Several Hercules C-130 cargo planes flew over one thousand miles beyond Israel's borders and landed in Entebbe. Once safely on the ground, the lead team of commandos proceeded to the terminal. Dressed to resemble the Ugandan dictator Idi Amin and his entourage, and riding in the type of black Mercedes he favored, the team from Sayeret Matkal drove to the terminal, stormed the passenger hall, and rescued the stunned hostages.

Entebbe was the last straw. The Mossad and Military Intelligence upgraded the importance of assassinating Dr. Wadi Haddad after the victorious mission. Haddad, however, resided in Baghdad and rarely traveled, complicating their work. In the spring of 1977, nearly one year after Entebbe, it was clear that the mountain would not come to Muhammad; the Mossad decided to bring Muhammad to the mountain. An assassination plan took shape and was authorized by newly inaugurated Prime Minister Menachem Begin.

Dr. Haddad had a weak point: his sweet tooth. The man loved good chocolate, Belgian chocolate, particularly; Tzomet, the human intelligence collection arm of the Mossad, was keen to capitalize on that weakness. The plan called for a reliable Palestinian agent, a member of Dr. Haddad's organization, to bring the doctor a gift of Belgian chocolates upon return from travels in Europe. The valuable gift, unattainable in Iraq in those years, was coated by Mossad specialists with a lethal biological poison. Tzomet had good reason to believe that the chocoholic would eat the creamy squares alone, unwilling to share the delectable gift. And so it was. The agent brought his boss the gift when he got back from Europe and the doctor gleefully devoured it—alone. Weeks later he began to lose weight. He lost his appetite. Blood tests showed that his immune system was compromised. It took him a few long months to die.

The faction under Dr. Wadi Haddad's command collapsed after his death. Dry statistics indicate that the number of attacks against Israeli targets abroad plummeted with his passing. Israeli intelligence and, in particular, the Mossad, viewed this as further proof of the effectiveness of their assassination program. The intelligence community presented these facts and conclusions to the new prime minister, explaining that the bio-hit on Haddad was the very definition of a preventive assassination, eradicating a ticking bomb, a man with a fertile mind who never stopped planning the next attack.

Menachem Begin was pleased with the execution and results of the Haddad assassination, and authorized yet another elimination, one that Mossad members somewhat arrogantly referred to as "something we just picked up . . ."

The target was Zuhir Mokhsan, head of the pro-Syrian Palestinian terror organization A-Tzaika. His assassination, in the summer of 1979, was not particularly complicated, and didn't require extensive intelligence gathering. Mokhsan, who did not take even minimal safety precautions, was shot on July 25, 1979, by two assassins from Caesarea's Kidon unit in the hallway of his apartment building in Cannes, on the French Riviera. Fatally injured, he died the next day at the Louis Pasteur Hospital in Nice. The French police announced that the murdered man had arrived in France with a Syrian diplomatic passport, claiming to have been born in Damascus. Mokhsan's sudden death led to the dissolution of the A-Tzaika organization—another veritable well of terrorism gone dry.

• • •

The numbers show a steep slide in the frequency of terror attacks against Israelis and Israeli institutions abroad from 1974 to the present. At the end of the 1970s, top-ranking Israeli intelligence officials were in near unanimous agreement that Israel's post-Munich wave of retaliatory and preventive assassinations gravely affected terrorist organizations, causing some to fold and others to limp. For Fatah and other groups that survived, the onslaught hindered their ability to function in Europe and deterred them from acting, forcing them to gradually abandon the idea of mega-attacks against Israeli targets abroad. That said, many in the Israeli intelligence community acknowledged that the Palestinians were also motivated by pragmatism. As time went on, the PLO realized that attacks outside Israel were doing their cause more harm than good.

On the Palestinian side, the leading consensus was to stand firm, which meant that the Mossad's assassinations had not deterred them, as General Aharon Yariv and others at Israeli intelligence agencies believed—or wanted people to believe. The explanation for the drop and the eventual cessation of foreign attacks, rather, could be found in the Palestinians' gradual transition from terrorism to political action and international diplomacy. This change peaked with Yasser Arafat's speech at the United Nations in New York in 1974. The Palestinians had labored for international recognition—terrorism had been a part of that fight. Now they had it. There was no longer a need for international terrorism—and it could damage their image.

Most of the Israeli intelligence community remains convinced that their campaign forced an end to overseas terror.

32 ALI HASSAN SALAMEH

Ali Hassan Salameh was philosophical about the matter of his death, telling *Time* magazine, "They're the ones who should be worried after all their mistakes. But I also know that when my number is up, it will be up. No one can stop it."

It had been more than five years since Salameh had been directly involved in terrorism; even Black September, the name used by Fatah, was no longer active. But ever since the lethal blunder in Lillehammer, the urge to eliminate Salameh had been tied less to cold calculation and more to the human desire to right a historical wrong. For Mike Harari and Caesarea, so long as he lived and breathed, Ali Hassan Salameh was a testament to their great failure. That black stain could be erased only with his death.

Even in the immediate wake of the Lillehammer disaster, the intelligence gathering in the hunt for Salameh never stopped. R., Caesarea's chief intelligence officer, pored over thousands of raw intelligence briefs looking for the man's Capture Point. Every relevant detail gleaned from the raw data was checked, analyzed, and filed.

Raw intelligence data showed that Salameh spent an inordinate amount of time practicing karate and pumping iron. He would go to the gym for hours at a time nearly every day. Undercover Caesarea combatants combed Beirut's gyms, putting miles on nearly every treadmill in the beleaguered city until they found their man. The Mossad operatives watched him carefully, noticing that he always hit the sauna before the shower. Soon, Mossad staff officers crafted a plan to plant a bomb under a sauna bench. The plan was discarded. There was no way to ensure that others would not join him at the last instant in the sauna or that the club wouldn't be severely damaged, perhaps putting more lives at risk.

Thousands of hours of manpower, in field and office, were devoted to the hunt for Salameh—it was one of Israeli intelligence's longest and most costly missions. HUMINT sources were asked time and again about the man, their ability to get close to him, his schedule, his habits, and his plans. The ears of Military Intelligence, Unit 8200, were instructed to intercept his calls or pick up any mention of his name. A new Mossad computer system searched satellite communication systems for the words "Ali Hassan Salameh" or "Abu-Hassan," recording all such conversations both in Israel and abroad. The Ali Hassan Salameh search, which was costly from a number of different perspectives, was a project the Mossad and Caesarea conducted with everything they had.

His name came up in covert meetings the Mossad conducted with Lebanese Christian Phalangist leaders, who were in close contact and even friendly with Salameh. They were asked very gently to keep the Mossad abreast of his actions. In March 1976, the Mossad held a secret meeting with Bashir Gemayel, the leader of the Christian forces in Lebanon, and Military Intelligence officers in the seaside Israeli town of Herzaliya. The future president of Lebanon was asked to provide details of Salameh's schedule and his daily routine. Gemayel promised to help, but his vow, like many of the Phalangists' promises, was hollow. Fulfilling it promised no foreseeable benefit.

• • •

Ali Hassan Salameh was born in 1942, the firstborn child of Hassan Salameh, an important gang leader in British Palestine. His father was notorious for his murderous zeal during the Jewish-Arab riots in the 1930s. By 1939, after the fall of the Great Arab Revolt, he was forced to flee Palestine, an enormous £10,000 bounty on his head. He traveled through Syria, Iraq, and Lebanon with his young wife before returning to Palestine. Two weeks after Prime Minister David Ben-Gurion declared independence, he fell in battle. A mortar shell pierced his lung as he led three hundred men in a charge on a village recently captured by Israel. He was thirty-seven.

Ali was only six years old when he lost his father. He lived with his mother, Um-Ali ("mother of Ali"), and two younger sisters, Nidal and Jihad, in Beirut. They lived in prosperity until Ali was sixteen and the family decided to leave tumultuous Lebanon—refugees a second time over. The young Ali Salameh had no interest in politics. He was rich, far removed from the people in the teeming Palestinian refugee camps around the Middle East longing for home and revenge.

He went to West Germany to study engineering. But studies were the least of his interests. Far from the eye of Um-Ali, he breathed in the best of what Europe had to offer—elegant restaurants, palatial hotels, glittery nightclubs. He was obsessive about fashion, wearing well-tailored, exclusively black suits. He liked the company of women, and they liked him. His good looks, Eastern charm, and hospitality worked like a honey trap for young German women. The playboy spent hours each day sculpting his body in the weight room and practicing karate, which he recommended to all.

In 1963, he abided by his mother's wishes and returned to Egypt to marry a simple young woman from the respected Husseini clan. Within a year he had his first son—Hassan, bestowing the title Abu-Hassan. But neither the wedding nor the birth of a child altered the habits of the narcissistic Ali Hassan Salameh. He remained a respected member of Cairo's party scene, reveling in the city's posh nightclubs till the early hours of the morning.

In 1976, at the height of his power and influence in Fatah, Salameh agreed to his only press interview. Speaking with Nadia Salti Stephan in Beirut, he spoke of growing up in the shadow of his father.

"The influence of my father has posed a personal problem for me. I grew up in a family that considered 'struggle' a matter of heritage which should be carried on by generation after generation. . . . My father was not the only one in the family to give his life for Palestine: some twelve young men in my family, mostly cousins, died in the 1940s. My upbringing was politicized. I *lived* the Palestinian cause. . . . When my father fell as a martyr, Palestine was passed on to me, so to speak. My mother wanted me to be another Hassan Salameh. . . . This had a tremendous impact on me. I wanted to be myself. . . . Even as a child, I had to follow a certain pattern of behavior. . . . I was made constantly conscious of the fact that I was the son of Hassan Salameh and had to live up to that."

Abu-Hassan joined the PLO prior to the occupation of the West Bank and Gaza Strip—a result of Israel's crushing victory in the Six Day War in June 1967. As a protégé of Arafat's, Salameh rose through the ranks with ease. The leader of the PLO saw him as kin, preferred not to notice Salameh's self-indulgent lifestyle, and appointed him commander of his personal guard, Force 17, apparently so named after the extension number in the PLO's headquarters in Beirut. Salameh spent as much time as he could with the *ra'is*. As son of the Palestinian Hassan Salameh, the *shahid* who had lost his life in battle against the Zionists, Ali wanted to go far.

When Ali Hassan Salameh was sitting for his interview, Israeli intelligence continued to grasp at straws. The civil war that erupted in Lebanon in 1975 worked both for and against the Mossad. On the one hand, deteriorating federal power made getting in and out of Beirut simple. On the other hand, the combatants were exposed to great risk in a lawless city with no rules and no judges, a regular rain of artillery and mortar fire, and the all-too-frequent sound of snipers' bullets. The risk of catching a stray or well-aimed sniper bullet, or of simply being mistaken for a tourist and mugged at gunpoint, perhaps taken for ransom, was too great. Many assassination plans went unfinished. Even innovative and elegant operations were sidelined out of concern for the combatants' safety. Most of the plans to kill Ali Hassan Salameh in the chaos of Beirut stopped at Mike Harari's door.

After Spring of Youth, Salameh had grown cautious about his personal safety, hiring dozens of armed security guards. In the aforementioned interview, Salameh was unsparing in his criticism of the three men slain during that operation. "The enemy's main victory—the assassination of three of our leaders in Beirut in April 1973—was the result of complete carelessness, which is typical of the Eastern mentality, the fatalistic mentality. My home was about fifty meters from the late Abu-Yussef's home. The Israeli assassins didn't come to my home for a very simple reason: it was guarded by my fourteen men."

There is something profound beneath his sharp sentiments. Unwittingly, Salameh too was taken in by the Mossad myth. That legend told of an Israeli organization so cunning and capable it could strike down any Palestinian in the world in his bedroom. Internalizing the myth, Salameh believed that the Mossad knew precisely where his apartment was in Beirut—fifty meters from Abu-Yussef's place—but was deterred by his fourteen armed guards, which they supposedly knew about. He never considered that the Israeli intelligence agency simply did not know where he lived, which explains why they never came to kill him that night.

Salameh tried to remain unpredictable in his habits. He kept loaded AK-47s in every room in his apartment. His boss, Yasser Arafat, was even more obsessive about safety, always maintaining an erratic schedule. He hardly ever spent two nights in the same bed. In an attempt to baffle potential assassins—both Israeli and other—he always left sleeping arrangements for the last minute. Although he was mentioned many times as a possible heir to Arafat, Ali Hassan Salameh was too lazy and far too devoted to luxury and pizzazz to abide by the gray edicts of purposefully erratic behavior.

His second marriage, this time in a white suit, only made him less cautious. In Beirut, on June 8, 1977, he married Georgina Rizak, a Christian Lebanese woman who had been crowned Miss Universe 1970. For Salameh, it was love at first sight, which hardly explains why he married the beautiful Rizak without divorcing his first wife, the mother of his two sons, Hassan and Osama. As a Muslim he was allowed more than one wife, he maintained. At any rate, Rizak kept him at home, night after night, in the Snobar section of west Beirut.

Salameh, thought to have been behind the Munich attack, was kept alive for years by virtue of his connection to the CIA. He was Arafat's liaison with the spy agency, a secret channel enabling communications between the Palestinian leader and the

American administration, which refused to publicly acknowledge the PLO. More than once, CIA operatives even offered to put Salameh on their payroll.

Up until the early 1970s the CIA was largely uninterested in the Palestinian side of the Arab-Israeli conflict. That changed after the brutal attack in Munich and, especially, after the execution of the two American diplomats in Khartoum at the hands of Fatah's Black September. The CIA sought ways to infiltrate Fatah—the largest of the Palestinian groups. The agency wanted someone who could both warn them of imminent attacks against Americans in Europe, the Middle East, and the increasingly perilous city of Beirut, and dissuade Fatah from pursuing such targets. Ali Hassan Salameh was the man for the job. The CIA first made contact with him in 1969, in Beirut. A friend of Salameh's introduced him to Robert C. Ames, a case officer working out of the American embassy in Lebanon. On at least two occasions CIA operatives offered Salameh a six-figure monthly salary to work as an agent. He refused. The American system—buying with vast sums of money—backfired with Salameh, wounding his pride. Salameh had no desire to be on the payroll; he wanted to change the thinking of the superpower that refused to recognize the legitimacy of the Palestinian cause.

From 1975 to 1976, during the early years of the civil war in Lebanon, the man affectionately know as "the Persuader," for his capacity to solve problems and assuage enemy minds, provided protection for the American embassy and its staff in Beirut. It was he who, on June 20, 1976, safeguarded the long convoy of embassy staff as they fled to Syria when fighting broke out on the streets of Beirut.

Salameh's connection with the Americans was on and off for ten years. He probably visited the United States twice: once as a member of Arafat's entourage, when the *ra'is* delivered his famous speech from the U.N.'s podium, and again in 1976, when he went undercover to meet high-ranking administration officials in Washington, and from there, with Rizak, at the time his girlfriend, to New Orleans and Hawaii. The trip, apparently on the CIA's generous tab, was part of their failed recruitment effort.

As far as Salameh was concerned, his connection with the Americans was his ace in the hole, his life insurance policy. The Americans would keep the Israelis at bay. But it was not that simple. The Israelis played with a different hand; his ace in the hole was useless. In May 1977 Prime Minister Menachem Begin came to power and reissued the authorization given by his predecessors to assassinate Ali Hassan Salameh.

In mid-1978 Mossad officials held a standard meeting with their American counterparts at CIA. "Did it ever work with Salameh?" a senior American official was asked, referring to the attempts at recruiting him.

"No," he said, shaking his head. "Everything failed . . ."

The Mossad interpreted this as a green light for assassination. Once the Americans had given up their efforts, they figured, he was fair game. The different branches of the American and Israeli intelligence agencies were already then in close contact. SIGINT, signal intelligence of telecommunications, was shared and efforts were made to ensure that HUMINT sources were not approached by both sides. Several times a year Mossad and CIA representatives convened for sessions on terrorism that went far beyond the everyday cooperation and exchange of information. The Americans would understand Israel's need to eliminate the terrorist.

From an Israeli perspective, Ali Hassan Salameh was one of the planners of Munich, period. Dozens of senior ex-Mossad and ex–Military Intelligence officers emphasized, over the course of our conversations, that the intelligence pointing to his involvement was both very strong and diverse. One senior officer told me that Salameh continued to plan terror attacks in Israel well after Munich and after the European theater quieted. Salameh, he said, was the man in Arafat's office who would translate the ideology into action, making the calls from headquarters to operatives in the field.

The Palestinians tell a different story. Both Abu-Daoud and Tawfiq Tirawi, a senior deputy of Abu-Iyad's and current head of the General Intelligence Apparatus in the West Bank, acknowledge a long litany of attacks orchestrated by Salameh in Europe, but categorically deny his involvement in the Munich attack. When speaking with Tirawi in his Ramallah office, he made clear to me that his intention is not to belittle Salameh's lifework, but to set the record straight. Salameh, though, was a braggart, unafraid of embellishing the truth. His bravado reached the Tzomet division and they duly reported that his hands were red with the blood of the murdered at Munich. The Israeli media crowned him "The Red Prince."

Salameh was responsible for four major terror attacks in Europe and one in Asia, according to Palestinian sources. The first, with the aid of Muhammad Boudia, on March 15, 1971, entailed the explosion of a 16,000-ton oil tank in Rotterdam. The second came on December 15, 1971, and involved a lone terrorist who waited in ambush for Ziad Al-Rifa'i, the Jordanian ambassador in London. Rifa'i was lightly wounded in his hand. The third attack was perpetrated in Cologne, Germany. On February 6, 1972, five young Palestinians with Jordanian passports— supposedly Mossad agents—were shot and killed. Half a year later, on August 4, 1972, he planned an attack along with Boudia that resulted in the blowing up of the oil storage tanks in Trieste, burning 200,000 gallons of oil used primarily by Germany. Then too Black September took responsibility for the attack. The fifth attack planned by Salameh was the unsuccessful takeover of the Israeli embassy in Bangkok in late December 1972. There, the terrorists agreed to be flown to Egypt empty-handed. Salameh was furious with the outcome, taking the lack of determination on the terrorists' part as a personal insult. There were some in Arafat's inner circle who took care to remind him of the failure in Bangkok now and again.

In conversations I had with senior ex-Caesarea officers they looked at their desire to kill Salameh in terms of closure—we want to "close the circle," they said. To set the record straight after the disaster in Lillehammer. The passing of time did not cool that desire: it intensified it. From 1972 onward many terrible attacks were carried out by Palestinian terrorists, claiming dozens of innocent lives, and yet no one hurried to draw Xs on the faces of those responsible. Few were added to the Mossad hit list. Salameh, despite a period of silence, never stopped being a top priority. "At that time, were there senior Palestinian activists more deserving of the opportunity to meet their creator than Ali Hassan Salameh?" I asked a senior Mossad officer. The reply: "Undoubtedly, yes." Despite the steep price invested, in terms of money, technological resources, and manpower, Caesarea's combatants remained devoted—the chase bordered on obsession.

In the second half of 1978 the noose began to tighten. A careful analysis of the abundant intelligence pouring in isolated a few weak points that could, with proper planning, be made into a Capture Point. Salameh was good about going to visit his mother and sisters. The Mossad recognized that in order to reach the building they shared he had to pass along the north–south route of Verdun Street. That was the Capture Point. In 1978, the

Mossad decided to send an undercover Caesarea combatant to Beirut. She, like Sylvia Raphael, worked for the Mossad part-time, only when asked.

Tel Aviv decided that the combatant, who had been trained well for her position in Caesarea, would take up residence in a flat in Beirut that overlooked Verdun Street and collect information about Ali Hassan Salameh. The combatant, exposed many years ago as Erika Chambers, came to Beirut in November 1978, carrying a British passport issued on May 30, 1975, number 25948. She made sure that her neighbors took note of her harmless eccentricities, painting wildly and feeding the neighborhood cats. Her cover: she was a worker at a Palestinian children's aid organization.

Chambers rented an apartment on the eighth floor of a luxury building on January 10, 1979. From her apartment in the Anis Assaf building she could see narrow Beka Street, into which Salameh turned on his afternoon journeys from his wife's flat. Chambers rented the place for three months, paying 3,500 Lebanese pounds up front. The Lebanese investigative report states that two foreign men, one Canadian and one British, entered the country with fake papers and passports. They were Caesarea combatants.

At 1525 hours, on January 22, 1979, Ali Hassan Salameh left his pregnant wife and got into the tan Chevrolet that waited for him with its motor running. Two bodyguards rode with him in the Chevy and two more climbed into the Land Rover following them. Salameh was on the way to his mother's house for the birthday party of his niece, Nidal's daughter, who turned three that day. A video camera had been purchased for the occasion.

The convoy slowly turned right onto the narrow Beka Street, where a rented Volkswagen waited on the left-hand side of the road, packed with eleven pounds of hexagene, a plastic explosive equal to seventy pounds of dynamite. One of the combatants stood a hundred yards away and watched the convoy approach. He flipped the switch on the detonator as the Chevrolet rolled past. The explosion rocked the whole block. An eyewitness described seeing a ball of fire and then hearing a deafening explosion. Cars lit up in flames and several bodies were strewn on the street, burned by the flames. One man stumbled out of the car and fell to the ground. People recognized him even in his current state—Abu-Hassan, Ali Hassan Salameh, they said. He was taken to the hospital, where he was pronounced dead.

Salameh's funeral was well attended. One memorable scene from that day: Hassan, the thirteen-year-old son of the *shahid*, sitting in Arafat's lap, an AK-47 in hand, a kaffiyeh similar to the one Arafat wore across his shoulders, and a military beret on his head. It seemed clear that he represented the third generation of armed struggle.

At twenty-nine, sixteen years after the funeral, Hassan returned to Palestine as a businessman and took up residence in Ramallah. Hassan Ali Salameh, educated in some of the best private schools in England, had a different take on life than that of his father and grandfather. "My father wanted me to be brought up away from his kind of life. I have a genuine desire for peace and I have a different mentality from the fighters of the past," he said.

33 "KEEP ME POSTED"

In autumn 1986 the members of the Target-Tracking Committee were called to the "Seminary," the Mossad's instructional facility. Located on a slight hill overlooking the sea, it was a place to which the military men, in flannel shirts and jeans, were always happy to come. Aside from the benefit of shedding their uniforms, they knew lunch would be world-class. The Mossad was famous for it. Many heads of state were received in the Seminary. Golda went there to relax after cancer treatments.

Each member of the five-person forum understood that a vital piece of raw intelligence regarding a major terrorist had come through the pipes. In an upstairs room, with the sea twinkling outside the window, they would be asked to analyze the intelligence and determine whether it was significant enough to put a person on, or off, the target list. Today's news was different. The Mossad Facha division head waited for everyone to take their place around the hardwood conference table before he let the news spill out. "They're all dead," he said of the terrorists responsible for the Munich Massacre. "None of them are breathing anymore."

Everyone wanted details, but the Facha chief wouldn't say another word. The committee members knew his announcement related to two of the three terrorists that had left the scene of the massacre alive. The Mossad had reported that the third man, Adnan Al-Jishey, had died of heart failure sometime in 1978–1979 in the Persian Gulf state of Dubai. His natural death, they were told, was caused by a genetic heart mutation. Now they learned that the circle had been closed—Jamal Al-Jishey and Mohammed Safady had also expired. All of the perpetrators of the murder had paid the price. The news was sent up the chain of command to Prime Minister Menachem Begin. Nothing was leaked to the press.

Khaled Abu-Toameh, an Israeli Arab journalist, had certainly not heard about the meeting. On July 31, 1992, he published an interview with Jamal Al-Jishey. The glaring headline over the front-page article in the weekly *Jerusalem* was: "Mossad Still Trying to Kill Me." Al-Jishey, forty, lived in Tunis and continued to abide by strict security precautions. "I'm sure the Mossad is still looking for me," he said. "As far as the Israelis are concerned, the case is not yet closed. The Mossad will try to kill me until the day I die."

An additional testament to Al-Jishey's sound health came in 2000, with the release of the Academy Award–winning documentary *One Day in September*. In Arthur Cohen's movie, Al-Jishey sits for long interviews, his face blackened and his form distorted by a hat.

The fate of Mohammed Safady, the third terrorist to leave Munich alive, remains ambiguous, although most analysts tended to believe he had been killed. Some members of the intelligence community intimated that his death had come at the hands of the Lebanese Christian Phalangists—Israel's allies—as a gesture of sorts to the Israeli Mossad. The *Jerusalem* article supported that notion, noting that Jamal Al-Jishey was the last man standing from the massacre. Tawfiq Tirawi disagrees. In a conversation we held in his Ramallah office in July 2005, Tirawi confirmed that he and Safady were close friends and that Safady was alive and well. "As alive as you are," Tirawi said, smiling playfully, refusing to add details. "The Israelis could still harm him," he explained.

Thought to be dead, Jamal Al-Jishey and Mohammed Safady were officially removed from the Israeli hit list in 1986, at the close of the meeting held in the Seminary. The permanent members of the committee were the head of Target Branch of Military Intelligence, a lieutenant colonel; the head of the Terror Division in Military Intelligence, a colonel; the head of the Intelligence Gathering Division in Military Intelligence, a colonel; the head of a branch of Unit 8200, Israel's high-quality NSA equivalent, a lieutenant colonel; and the host of the meeting, the head of the Facha division at the Mossad, the equivalent of a major general. "The Mossad member was always someone serious, a former combatant, very mission-oriented," one of the regular members told me. "The list itself had a maximum of fifteen slots. Over the years, two or three names were taken off the list and replaced by others after it became clear that the person was not involved in Munich. Others were added when information implicated them in the attack. Some kept their borderline status the whole time."

The meetings went straight to the point. "We addressed only new intelligence. Usually one of the agencies had new information about a wanted man, something like upcoming travel plans. Once we all agreed that the information was credible, we shifted gears, becoming more focused, active, and secretive. The Mossad would then bring in Caesarea's chief intelligence officer. He and his staff officers would organize and collect all of the intelligence information, including pictures of the target, and the target buildings, from the ground and from above. As the plans progressed, the attention to detail increased. At this stage we were all in operation mode."

The head of the Mossad brought the finalized plan to the Heads of Agencies Committee. There, the heads of the Mossad, Shabak, and Military Intelligence, frequently joined by the military aide to the prime minister, could debate the necessity or timing of a mission, arguing for its suspension or delay. Only the prime minister had veto power. The need for these meetings was purely practical. The 1995 assassination of Fatkhi Shkaki illustrates their utility.

As head of the Palestinian Islamic Jihad, a small, extreme terrorist organization, Fatkhi Shkaki proved himself quite able. He was a strong leader with a firm grip on every aspect of his organization. In January 1995, after a deadly attack at Beit Lid junction east of the Israeli city of Netanya, it was decided to begin planning his assassination. The goal was preventive—it was assumed that eliminating the capable Shkaki would keep Islamic Jihad out of action for a year or two.

Prime Minister Yitzhak Rabin authorized the commencement of operational assassination plans. For roughly two months the Mossad collected intelligence on Shkaki, filling his already fat file with even more information. The intensive intelligence-gathering effort bore fruit. Shkaki could be killed in early summer 1995. They presented their plan and the proof of his guilt to the agency heads.

Uri Saguy, head of Military Intelligence, was dead set against the Mossad plan. After the meeting he spoke with Prime Minister

Rabin, explaining that the assassination, which was to be carried out in the heart of Damascus, would damage the already shaky, ongoing Israeli-Syrian peace negotiations. Saguy asked that the operation be moved to a different locale, somewhere neutral, a place that would not impact the chance of peace. Rabin accepted his argument. He instructed the Mossad to change their plans.

Shkaki, a terrorist with the blood of dozens of Israelis on his hands, a man with a bulldozer-like ability to get things done in the world of organized terrorism, lived in Damascus, and rarely left. Shabtai Shavit, the head of the Mossad, and others in the organization were forced to accept Rabin's decision. Their plan, tailor-made for Damascus and ready to be executed at a moment's notice, had to be shelved, perhaps indefinitely.

The Mossad continued to collect intelligence on Shkaki, learning his routine and paying special attention to his travel plans. They needed a clean plan, something that would leave no Israeli prints. They learned that when Shkaki did leave Damascus, it was to one of two places—Tehran, on a direct flight, or Libya, which he reached either by ferry, via Malta, or plane, via Tunis. The Mossad chose the island of Malta. Saguy and the prime minister were pleased. All they had to do was wait. Once Caesarea was given the go-ahead, operations were frozen eight different times; once, out of a sudden concern for the assassins' well-being just thirty seconds before they pulled the trigger. On October 28, 1995, Shkaki was shot dead outside the Diplomat Hotel in Malta. His killers, two combatants from Kidon, Caesarea's assassination wing, fled the scene on a motorcycle, and left the country immediately.

Israeli prime ministers had the power to take someone's life with a nod of their head. The way those decisions were addressed often revealed a great deal about a leader's character. They were far from the public eye when they met the heads of Mossad and they knew that nothing they said or did would be leaked to the public. The prime minister could, and did, act according to his or her conscience and worldview. Rabin was a ponderer, asking pesky and prying questions. He was pedantic, had a phenomenal memory, and demanded solid answers. He often sent Military Intelligence and Mossad officials packing. "It hasn't matured," he'd say in his slow baritone, leaving everyone to wonder if the timing was poor politically, the indictment insufficiently strong, or the man insufficiently guilty.

The routine has been the same since Golda. The prime minister is given a top secret file with a picture of the proposed target, some background data, and a densely worded, multi-paged indictment. Most prime ministers avoided reading the indictment, skipping straight to the recommendation, which, of course, always urged death.

At times intelligence information failed to translate into explicit guilt, but in the case of Munich, each prime minister, from Golda Meir to Yitzhak Rabin, by way of Menachem Begin, Yitzhak Shamir, and Shimon Peres, thought that the vengeful killing of *saya'an*s and terrorists alike was the proper response to that dreadful massacre. Not one of them said "let it go." Most of them never even asked the basic questions: Does this activist, implicated in the Munich Massacre, still have a role in terror attacks? Is he a threat today? Palatable words and titles like "logistical terror assistant" and "architect" were created, and would be found in the recommendation section of the indictments handed to the prime minister. But "architect" could easily refer to someone who once said something along the lines of "Italy could be a good place for an attack now." For that, he could pay with his life.

Prime Minister Menachem Begin trusted "our boys." He did

not examine details. Shimon Peres, in contrast, fired off numerous questions. He was not fond of assassination missions. That
changed in 1996. At the time he was in an election campaign
against right-wing Likud Party candidate Benjamin Netanyahu.
During the three months leading up to the election, Islamic Jihad
and Hamas carried out numerous deadly bus bombings and
other terror attacks, claiming many Israeli lives and taking a toll
on the national mood. Peres feared a high-profile attack on the
eve of the elections, certain to sink his chances of winning. Peres
turned to the Mossad. He asked them to prepare assassination
missions that could be ready to go at a moment's notice, carried
out within twenty-four hours. He ruled out Syria (diplomatic negotiations) and Jordan (a close neighbor and friend), leaving only
second-tier countries. Caesarea, displeased with the nature of the
task, prepared a number of missions, targeting *saya'an*s. In the
end, there was no attack and no Israeli response.

Yizhak Shamir was the easiest prime minister to work with.
As a former member of the Lechi, the pre-state Jewish underground, and of the Mossad, Shamir reveled in the details, and
avoided political excuses. He never said, "I'm going to Paris for a
diplomatic visit next week and it would be improper for there to
be a mission there concurrently." He was willing to authorize.
One of the few times he refused to do so was in December 1987.
Shamir was in the hospital at the time. Caesarea was in a good
position to assassinate a senior member of Ahmed Jibril's Popular Front for the Liberation of Palestine—General Council
(PFLP-GC). The man, allegedly responsible for numerous attacks
against Israel, was on the hit list and the assassins were in place.
Shabtai Shavit went to the hospital, seeking Shamir's approval.
When he returned, he told the expectant Mossad officers that
Shamir had not been in the mood to talk about it, granting the
PFLP-GC operative his life.

Each prime minister's military aide could receive all transmissions and codes as they were issued over the course of a mission in a very high-tech twenty-four-hour operations room. Prime ministers responded differently as missions unfolded. Some said, "Keep me posted." Others, "Let me know when it's over."

34 A KILLER FROM WITHIN

The annals of history will record a strange scene in the theater of the absurd that can define the Israeli-Palestinian conflict. The notorious terrorist Abu-Iyad, responsible for the Munich Massacre and other bloody attacks, was assassinated in Tunis in January 1991 — not by Israeli assassins after a dogged two-decade chase, but rather by one of his own bodyguards, out of an ideological conviction that Abu-Iyad was overly conciliatory toward Israel. The killer, recruited by Abu Nidal's group, a cruel and reactionary organization, was ordered to assassinate Abu-Iyad not long after he declared that a Palestinian state should rise alongside Israel, and not in place of it.

Salah Khalaf, better known as Abu-Iyad, was one of the key figures in internal Palestinian politics. He, along with Yasser Arafat, was one of the founding fathers of Fatah. Early on, Abu-Iyad was considered a militant and a hard-liner, advocating an unflinching campaign of terrorism and violence against Israel and Jordan. As head of the United Security Apparatus he guided a cadre of young Palestinian operatives through the ranks, gaining their enduring admiration and devotion—men such as Fakhri Al-Omri, Atef Bseiso, Amin Al-Hindi, and Tawfiq Tirawi.

Since the mid-1960s, Fatah's earliest days, Abu-Iyad had been responsible for terror operations that claimed the lives of many Israelis, including the Olympic attack, remembered as the Munich Massacre. Despite his denials of both culpability and involvement in Black September, Abu-Iyad topped Israel's Most Wanted list. Israel was driven by preventive considerations—to permanently halt the agile mind of the former philosophy teacher, who continuously conjured new and innovative attacks, always seeing them to fruition. The Israelis also wanted to make it clear to the terrorist activists and leaders that they were hunted for their sins, hoping to deter them and others from joining their ranks. Finally, and most important, the Israelis wanted to punish him, to exact revenge for Munich. Every Israeli intelligence officer dreamed of commanding the mission that would put Abu-Iyad six feet underground.

Abu-Iyad, a Palestinian, born in the city of Jaffa in 1933, remembered, even took pride, in the close ties his family had with Jews in Palestine during the 1940s. His father spoke Hebrew, he said. One day before Israel declared its independence, his family fled on a small ship to Egypt-controlled Gaza, instantly becoming refugees along with hundreds of thousands of Palestinians. The day of flight was imprinted in the memory of the fifteen-year-old youth.

A world-class orator, he would draw Palestinian crowds out of their seats even as he was seen ascending a podium. There was nothing in his appearance to suggest a fighter or a revolutionary, nor did he cultivate such an image. He was short, chubby, and solid; his face was round and full, his eyes were framed with bushy black eyebrows, and his thin, combed-back hair and mustache were graying. His dress was firmly middle-class, preferring an untailored blazer to the army uniform worn by Arafat and mimicked by many.

He knew his life was in constant danger, and not just from Tel Aviv. The Mukhabarat, a generic name for Arab nations' notorious internal secret-police apparatuses, sought to incapacitate him too. Jordan led the charge. Abu-Iyad was responsible for numerous assassination plans and several actual attempts to kill Jordan's monarch, King Hussein. He spearheaded the operation in Khartoum to liberate Abu-Daoud, the grandiose plan to topple the king and initiate a revolution in Jordan in February 1972, and an assassination attempt on King Hussein at the Rabat Conference in Morocco in 1974, which was foiled with the help of a Mossad tip that was passed to Jordan through Moroccan intelligence.

Abu-Iyad took precautions. Four armed guards took turns protecting him. But his fears only increased with time. In the spring of 1973, he heard his peers gunned down in the middle of the night by IDF forces during the Spring of Youth operation. In the late 1970s a feud developed between the PLO and the Egyptian administration once the latter signed a peace agreement with Israel, turning its back on the Palestinian problem. His relationship with Syrian president Hafez Al-Assad was testy as well; Abu-Iyad attacked him repeatedly in his oratory.

Abu-Iyad lived the life of the persecuted—far from his wife and six children, far from their suburban Cairo home, and without a permanent address. When he arrived at Fatah's offices, it was always without advance notice and accompanied by a posse of armed guards.

In *Stateless*, Abu-Iyad describes an attempt on his life in August 1973. As he tells it, he was working in the study of his Cairo home when a bodyguard interrupted him. There was a young Palestinian at the door; he insisted on delivering his message to Abu-Iyad personally. "I couldn't refuse him," Abu-Iyad writes. "As soon as he entered, he told me he had been sent to kill me, opening his attaché case and pulling out a pistol and a silencer. The young man said he had decided to confess out of fear of arrest or being killed during the assassination. In return, he asked that I keep him safe. He wanted to start a new life in one of the North African Arab countries; if that was impossible, then in one of the Socialist-bloc states. He said he was a Palestinian from the West Bank and his mission to kill me had been given to him by an Israeli security officer whose name he gave. After he had crossed the Jordan River on his way to Amman, where he was supposed to get on a plane, he was stopped by Jordanian police and taken in for questioning. After his mission was discovered, one of King Hussein's officers, Falah Al-Rifa'i, promised him an extra cash prize if he succeeded in killing me."

The Palestinian agent, allegedly recruited by the Israelis, was a double agent for the Jordanians. It was not a classic double-cross, rather a unique Middle Eastern phenomenon where a unity of interests in the war against Palestinian terror converged. The Israelis did not really care at whose behest their agent planned on killing Abu-Iyad, or for what additional sum of money.

According to the Palestinian double agent, he had received information about Abu-Iyad's residence, his Egyptian security detail, and his daily routine. The agent confessed that he was supposed to kill Abu-Iyad two days earlier, at the entrance to the government radio station. Abu-Iyad, the hunted, thanked the young man profusely, but remained circumspect. He took the man's contact information and said he would be in touch soon.

The plot thickened when the Egyptian Mukhabarat was asked by Abu-Iyad to enter the picture. During a covert search of the man's room they discovered several suspicious items, including a small, hermetically sealed suitcase that they could not pry open. "Three days later, at 0700, one of the bodyguards wakes me to tell me that the same youth wants to see me immediately. My curiosity was piqued and I agreed to meet him. Immediately when he entered the guest room I noticed that he was carrying the small suitcase that the Egyptian policemen described to me. I demanded that he open the suitcase immediately. He turned pale as plaster, murmuring, and, finally, breaking. He confessed to me that the suitcase held enough explosives to destroy the whole house and to kill my wife and six children. He had been instructed to hide the explosive device under the couch before he left. The first visit and the confession were to gain my trust and get familiar with the place before executing the second and final stage of the operation, as planned by the Israeli and Jordanian security forces. I turned him over to the Egyptian police. Till this day, he sits in a Cairo jail."

Abu-Iyad claims that twice his children were given boxes of chocolate that were connected to explosive devices. "To our good fortune, my wife and I taught our children to be alert. They are so suspicious that they don't even open candy packages that I send with somebody to hand-deliver to them when I am abroad."

The Israelis hunted Abu-Iyad for years to no avail. Abu-Iyad did not travel to Europe, his schedule followed no observable routine, and he kept a cadre of guards around him at all times. After the Palestinian leadership was expelled from Lebanon by the Israelis in 1982, he relocated to Tunis, and remained there, rarely venturing beyond its borders. "We were very close to Abu-Iyad a number of times but we had to stop in our tracks because the risk to the combatants on the ground was too great or we lacked a solid operational scheme," Colonel (res.) Yossi Daskal, the former head of the Terror Division at Military Intelligence, told me.

But for Daskal, a veteran officer, a professional used to making cost-benefit analyses with human lives on the line, the chase may not have been worthwhile. "The hunt for people no longer central to terror rings and operations puts a burden on the collection wings of our intelligence agencies. Many Mossad *katsa*s spent a lot of time looking for information on these people."

Abu-Iyad, in stark contrast to his peers, the founding fathers of Fatah, softened his stance on Israel over the years. In February 1974, he was the first to publicly declare the need to establish a Palestinian state on less than the entirety of their homeland, alongside the state of Israel. In August 1988, he was still far ahead of his time in declaring his willingness to accept the state of Israel alongside the Palestinian state that was to come. "If you give me the West Bank and Gaza—I will take it; and if you give me less than that—I will take it too."

This slide into moderation angered Palestinian extremists. Chief among them was Sabri Al-Bana, aka Abu Nidal, a sadistic zealot. He led a group of loyal followers called the Revolutionary Council of Fatah. The group, which sometimes called itself by the more catchy name "Black June," assassinated moderate Palestinian officials in Europe and across the Middle East. Abu Nidal claimed it was his duty to save the Palestinian resistance movement from Arafat and his colleagues who had strayed from the path of liberating all of Palestine through armed struggle. Abu Nidal's organization murdered at least sixteen Palestinians he deemed too moderate. He branched out on occasion. In 1976, under pressure from Iraqi vice president Saddam Hussein, his organization tried to assassinate the president of Syria, Hafez Al-Assad, Saddam Hussein's bitter rival.

Another deviation took place on June 3, 1982, when Abu Nidal sent men to kill Shlomo Argov, the Israeli ambassador to

Britain. That act was used by Prime Minister Begin and his defense minister, Ariel Sharon, as an alleged final straw that demanded an Israeli invasion of Lebanon. The invasion grew into the Lebanon War and devolved into a two-decades-long guerrilla conflict.

Abu Nidal's cruelty was legendary. Myths and stories circulated through the ranks of Fatah. People claimed the man enjoyed killing. One of his favorite execution techniques was to place a bound victim inside a pit and then pour concrete into the hole, burying the man alive.

One of Abu Nidal's final missions was the assassination of Abu-Iyad and his close aide Fakhri Al-Omri on January 14, 1991, the day before the first Gulf War commenced. Operation Desert Storm overshadowed the event. On the evening before the war officially commenced Abu-Iyad and Fakhri Al-Omri, a man also thought to be deeply involved in the planning and execution of the Munich attack, had dinner at the Tunis home of Ha'il Abed el-Hamid, aka Abu-el-Hul, a close friend and top operations officer for the Western Wing (charged with carrying out attacks in Israel) of Fatah. Over dinner, they discussed Saddam Hussein's brutal conduct in Kuwait, Arafat's support of the Iraqi dictator, and the imminent invasion by the allied force. Everything proceeded smoothly until close to midnight, when Hamza Abu-Zaid, a simple bodyguard, walked into the living room, where the three sat, smoking and drinking. He passed a note to Abu-Iyad and made his way back to the door. Without warning he spun around and opened fire with the automatic weapon in his hand, killing all three men. He tried to escape, but was stopped, jailed, and later executed. Abu-Zaid, a Fatah operative, had been secretly recruited by Abu Nidal's people and tasked with killing the traitor.

So fell Abu-Iyad, the man more responsible than any other for the Munich Massacre, by the hand of a compatriot, for his dovish views. Israel received the news with ambivalence. On the one hand, he was responsible for the murder of innocent Israelis; on the other, he had gone where few dared on the Palestinian side, offering the possibility of diplomatic negotiations between Israel and the Palestinians. In January 1991 diplomatic negotiations between the two warring sides sounded like a pipe dream, but after the war, in October of that year, they met in Madrid, Spain. Israeli and Palestinian delegations sat face-to-face in what was the official beginning of diplomatic negotiations.

As fate would have it, the security officer of the Palestinian delegation was Atef Bseiso, Abu-Iyad's protégé, who, in his role as Fatah's liaison officer with European secret services, tended to the security of the Palestinian delegation.

35 CROSSING THE JORDAN

On Thursday morning, March 28, 1996, Mohammed Oudeh, better known as Abu-Daoud, the man who twenty-four years earlier planned and commanded the Munich attack, walked—slowly and ceremoniously—over the Allenby Bridge, crossing from Jordan into Israel. Abu-Daoud entered the joint Israeli-Palestinian terminal. He shook hands with an Israeli colonel before entering the office of a Shabak representative, who verified his documents and sized him up, interviewing him about his future plans. At the Israeli border crossing he was secretly photographed from several angles, entering the Israeli defense establishment's archives as he filled out application forms for a Palestinian ID card. He accepted a temporary ID document and made his way to the VIP room, where he fell into the arms of Tawfiq Tirawi. Tirawi kissed him on both cheeks before ushering him into one of a fleet of BMWs. They drove southwest, toward Gaza, where Yasser Arafat and many other Fatah colleagues had their offices. Abu-Daoud had not seen these men in two years, since May 1994, when the PLO signed the Oslo Accords with Israel, allowing, among other things, the return of Fatah activists to Gaza and the West Bank.

In the spacious leather interior of the BMW, Abu-Daoud fretted. Maybe the Israelis were waiting. Maybe they would let him get to the gates of Gaza and then arrest him for his role in the Olympic attack. He, the wanted murderer, as the Israelis called him, the terrorist who admitted to his pivotal role in the attack, had shaken hands and made small talk with Israeli officers. Who would have believed it? He smiled— So far, so good, he thought. He was in Palestine, preparing to take part in the most momentous period in his homeland's history. For twenty-four years he had been on the run, afraid of Israel's long reach, looking over his shoulder, fearing a Mossad assassin at his back. For twenty-four years he got into bed not knowing if he would wake up in the morning. Al-Yahud, the Jews had tried to kill him several times. They might well try again.

Abu-Daoud's arrival was coordinated and prearranged. He came to Palestine just before the Palestinian National Council convened. They were set to eradicate the article in their charter calling for the destruction of the state of Israel. The authorization of Abu-Daoud's entry to the Palestinian-controlled areas came from deep within the corridors of power—Shimon Peres signed off on the decision. The prime minister claimed that Abu-Daoud's entry, like that of numerous other high-level terrorists, offered two benefits: one, Abu-Daoud would play a role in annulling the charter calling for Israel's destruction; two, Peres felt it was better for men like Abu-Daoud to take up residence in Gaza, where terrorism was being renounced, rather than in Damascus, where it was supported.

Once in Gaza, Abu-Daoud met with old Fatah friends, interested to see what sort of senior position they had reserved for him as payment for his service to homeland and organization. Abu-Daoud received a Palestinian passport/laissez-passer and a green Palestinian ID card, printed and prepared by the state of Israel, number 410448807.

But Abu-Daoud had stepped on too many toes and the loot—the financial monopolies and the government posts—had already been taken by Arafat and his cronies in the Palestinian Authority. No one was willing to offer him the payment he sought for his years of service. After three years in his homeland, Abu-Daoud chose to exile himself. On June 2, 1999, he left Palestine, angered and embittered, through the Rafah crossing to Egypt. He settled in Damascus, to finish his memoirs.

In 2003, Abu-Daoud's passport/laissez-passer was renewed by Israel. Two years later, almost sixty-eight years old, Abu-Daoud sent a formal request, via Palestinian Authority Minister of Internal Affairs Muhammad Dahlan, to return to Palestine. "He wants to come back to be buried in Palestine. It's his last wish," a friend explained. The Israelis sent a succinct message back to Dahlan—it's best for all involved that he not show up at the bridge. Abu-Daoud could have shown up at the border crossing at any time, presented his passport to the Israeli officers, and continued to the Palestinian-controlled areas. The signed agreements guaranteed his safety from Israeli prosecutors and prisons—he had a Palestinian ID card and passport. Nor could they arrest him for the thirty-three-year-old massacre. The Israeli-Palestinian Interim Agreement on the West Bank and Gaza Strip, signed by Yasser Arafat and Yitzhak Rabin in Washington on September 28, 1995, clearly states on page 19, under the title "Confidence Building Measures," Article XVI, Section 3, that a "Palestinian from abroad whose entry into the West Bank and the Gaza Strip is approved pursuant to this Agreement, and to whom the provisions of this article are applicable, will not be prosecuted for offenses committed prior to September 13, 1993." Moreover,

Abu-Daoud had not been involved in terrorist activity in roughly twenty years, thus forbidding Israel from barring his entry or stripping him of his Palestinian citizenship. Though well aware of the law, the Israeli government hoped that Abu-Daoud's enduring fear of assassination would convince the old man not to present himself at the border. No one in Israel needed the embarrassment of his return, least of all Shimon Peres, who had let him in the first time around.

The source of Abu-Daoud's deep-seated suspicion was the unshakable fear he lived with from 1972 to 1996. Up until the mid-1970s he was deeply involved in planning terror attacks. In February 1973, four months after the Munich Massacre, he was arrested in Amman, Jordan, his design to overthrow the king foiled. Abu-Daoud received a death sentence, which was mitigated to life in prison. Several months later, the politically astute king, who ruled over a country where 60 percent of the populace was Palestinian, pardoned him altogether.

An attempt on his life was made in Warsaw, on August 2, 1981. A lone assassin walked into the Hotel Intercontinental's restaurant, spotted Abu-Daoud, and fired five shots. The hit was amateurish: the weapon most probably used in the assassination attempt was found nearby; the assassin acted alone, in contrast to professional assassins, who work in pairs, covering each other; and the target was shot in the stomach and chest, not the head, which guarantees death. Nonetheless, Abu-Daoud was seriously injured and taken to a local hospital, where multiple life-saving surgeries were performed. The man with nine lives survived yet once more. Several weeks later he was transferred to a hospital in East Germany, where he began his rehabilitation. Abu-Daoud stayed in East Berlin till the fall of the Communist regime. In 1990, after years of preferential treatment, he left for Tunis and made his way to Syria.

Today, Abu-Daoud, like so many Palestinians, is still convinced that the Mossad, with its long reach, elephantine memory,
and unwillingness to forgive, was behind the attempt on his life.
That is part of the myth that both Israelis and Palestinians believe
in. But the assassination attempt in Warsaw was probably executed by Abu Nidal's agents or another adversarial group within
the PLO. It was not the Mossad that came to kill him.

For years after the assassination attempt Abu-Daoud went by
the name Tariq and lived comfortably behind the Iron Curtain in
East Germany, Poland, and Bulgaria. During that period it was
nearly impossible for the Mossad to reach him; his name was
hardly ever mentioned in the assassination forums.

In early January 1977, three and a half years before the assassination attempt in Warsaw, less than five years after the Munich
Massacre, the Paris police were forced to arrest Abu-Daoud. In
France to attend a friend's funeral, he carried a forged Iraqi passport with the name Yousef Raji Hanna. His entry visa had been
inserted by officials at the French consulate in Beirut, as part of a
PLO delegation. His presence and his cover were leaked. West
Germany formally requested his extradition, hoping to try him in
the still pending case of the murder of Israeli athletes at the Munich Olympics. Israel issued no such appeal. Bereaved family
members of the athletes issued a private extradition request to
the French embassy signed by a lawyer. A widely publicized picture of the children of the murdered athletes holding pictures of
their dead fathers made little impression on the French authorities. They released Abu-Daoud, whisking him off to Algeria,
where he received a hero's welcome. The French government explained its actions: the West German request had not arrived in
time.

According to a distinguished well-placed person who lived through the era and has taken part in shaping Israeli policy, the fact that Abu-Daoud is alive today is an Israeli failure, a blight on the defense establishment. "He should have been killed for his role in Munich," this person argued, "but too many people were insufficiently determined to follow through." Abu-Daoud, and two of the perpetrators of the massacre, are still alive. The mission was never fully accomplished, nor will it ever be. Their names were taken off the list a long time ago; today, their files sit in the Mossad archive, collecting dust.

EPILOGUE

Israel's intention after the Munich Massacre was to strike back at Fatah's senior Black September officials, to identify and kill those who had sent the murderous squad to Munich—as well as anyone else who persistently targeted Israelis abroad. That message, delivered with a bullet or a bomb, would, it was hoped, deter and hinder terrorist capabilities, and, certainly, satisfy Israel's thirst for revenge and punishment. Munich was the trigger, and for many years, assassination became a new tool in the war on terror.

However, members of the intelligence community soon realized that despite their unwavering devotion to the cause, which they saw as a mission of national importance, they were unable to exact a price from the top-level leaders. Men like Abu-Daoud, the commander of the Munich mission, and Abu-Iyad, deputy to Arafat and the true architect of the Olympic terror attack, remained beyond reach, unscathed. The combination of poor intelligence-gathering capacities on the one hand, and the flight of top leaders underground on the other, made operational plans against them nearly impossible. When, on rare occasions, the Mossad was ready to go, the risk to Caesarea combatants suspended the mission, often at the last minute.

The inability to strike back at Fatah's top Black September leaders was at odds with the rousing calls, from the defense establishment, the Knesset, and, primarily, the public, to settle the score. A compromise of sorts was born from this untenable situation: the government agreed to allow the Mossad and Military Intelligence to conduct their target search a few notches beneath the Fatah's shrouded upper echelons, thereby enabling a seemingly fitting response, but one that, from 1972 to 1973, claimed the lives of numerous low-level, easily accessible activists—along with the more significant targets killed during Operation Spring of Youth.

Those targeted during those years were not directly connected to the Munich Massacre. Yet they were profiled in ways that implied direct culpability. One would be presented, through leaks to the media, as the "senior Black September representative in Paris," another as the "Black September leader in Italy." Such titles not only satisfied the prime minister's and the nation's desire for revenge and resolution, but also eased the bitterness of the pill that European nations were forced to swallow, as Israel, with considerable chutzpah, disregarded their sovereignty time and again.

In those days, the Israeli public preferred to sidestep the question of whether or not it was just to kill Wael Zu'aytir, the translator of *One Thousand and One Nights*. The public's faith in the Israeli defense establishment was unwavering. Everyone bought into the evolving myth of the Mossad's infallibility. The Mossad always got their man; if someone was found dead, then they must be guilty. The myth was so potent that it spread to the Palestinian Diaspora. An assassinated Palestinian, even someone thought to be completely outside the fray of the armed struggle, was immediately elevated to the status of hero of the armed Palestinian resistance. The Mossad, after all, had taken the trouble to track him and kill him hundreds of miles from home.

The myth's power grew exponentially in Palestinian minds after Operation Spring of Youth. Israel's ability to attack and kill Arafat's deputy in his own bedroom left an indelible mark on all terrorists and activists. The threat of a sudden death followed them everywhere. Not even the incompetent and fatal blunder in Lillehammer could diminish the Mossad's aura of invincibility.

Thousands of officers, analysts, and combatants in the Mossad and Military Intelligence had no doubt that, in their pursuit of Palestinian activists, they were fulfilling the will of their people and were embarked on a mission of supreme national importance—spearheading the war on Palestinian terrorism. As events unfolded, they believed in their hearts that the assassinations they carried out were worthy acts, the evidence of guilt always sufficient to warrant death. The climate was different then. The covert operatives of the Mossad and Military Intelligence had been chosen to deliver justice in a distant land—and their eagerness to act was extraordinary.

As the desire to avenge the murder of the athletes subsided, the utility of assassinations—if not their justness, which is well beyond the scope of this book—became clear. Assassinations were seen as the reason that Palestinian terror grew silent in Europe. Buoyed by their success, Israel used the same tool in Lebanon in the 1980s.

For twenty years, almost no public cost-benefit analyses were conducted on the subject of assassinations. In 1992, Israeli air force helicopters fired hellfire missiles into the car of Abbas Musawi, head of the Shiite terrorist organization Hezbollah; Hezbollah responded, two months later, with an attack on the AMIA building in Argentina, claiming 196 lives. Deterrence had become a two-way street, and now a public debate erupted over whether assassinating the heads of terrorist organizations was worth it. In January 1996 Israeli agents assassinated "The Engineer," Yihya Ayash, a man responsible for countless terror attacks and one of the fathers of the tactic of suicide bombing. Hamas, the Palestinian terror organization he belonged to, responded with multiple bombings. Again, the public debated whether Ayash's assassination was worth the price. When there was no reprisal, there was no discussion. In 1995, Mossad combatants killed Fatkhi Shkaki, head of Islamic Jihad. There was no counterattack—the organization was paralyzed for years—and no debate.

The justness, efficacy, and value of assassinations have been debated throughout the current conflict. Strike and counterstrike have come in rapid succession. The debate, ebbing and flowing, remains unresolved.

APPENDIX: THE KOPEL REPORT

The fifteen-page top secret report came out in only three copies. Pinchas Kopel, Moshe Kashti, and Avigdor Bartel did exactly as Golda had asked: the anemic report refrained from accusing anyone of negligence or demanding the dismissal of any high-ranking officials and officers. Instead, Kopel and company passed the buck to the head of the Shabak. He, the report suggested, "can draw conclusions, as he sees fit, about those officials who are singled out in this report for unbecoming conduct in all matters concerning the security and safety of the Olympic delegation, as it was defined before the Munich disaster."

The report concluded, "The organizational structure and existing procedures of security for Israeli delegations abroad are not sufficient to address the current situation. Therefore, it is suggested that a new department be created in the Shabak to exclusively handle all matters of official security abroad. The new department will serve as the sole organization charged with dispensing advice and providing security for delegations as the government sees fit." The Kopel Report dryly conveys the chain of events that led to the security failures in Munich.

When a few, minimal conclusions from the report were talked about, it drew fire from the Knesset and the press. Many columnists and politicians expected an earthquake: they received a tremor. Yosef Harmelin, head of the Shabak, recommended the termination of employment for the embassy security officer in Bonn, Germany, and two security officers in the Shabak, including the commander of the security division.

To the grieving families the measures were insufficient. At the special parliamentary session convened after the massacre, Ilana Romano, the widow of Yossef Romano, turned to Deputy Prime Minister Yigal Allon and asked him what the government planned to do about the Israeli security lapses. Allon informed her that three security officials had been removed from their posts. When asked to clarify whether removed meant fired or rotated through the system, Allon answered admonishingly, "Would you like to see their families starve?"

Despite pressure, the report was never made public. It was sent to be buried in the state archives. Accounts of its conclusions and general tone varied wildly. Some columnists labeled it scathing, others bland and lukewarm. Twenty years after the massacre, in the summer of 1992, Ankie Spitzer and Ilana Romano met with Prime Minister and Defense Minister Yitzhak Rabin in his office in Tel Aviv. Spitzer asked Rabin to see the classified report, promising that she would read it to satisfy her own curiosity, but refrain from divulging its contents. "The report is important to me," she says. "I wanted to know how the Israeli authorities addressed the failures." Having never seen the contents of the report, Rabin asked his chief of staff, Eitan Haber, to hunt it down in the state archives, look it over, and recommend a course of action. At a different meeting several weeks later the matter of the report was brought up again. Haber told Spitzer that he would not be willing to show her so as much as its cover.

For the next thirteen years, the report lay undisturbed in the archives. In early 2005, thirty-two years after it was written, I issued a formal request to the manager of the state archives in Jerusalem to examine the Kopel Report. I received a negative response. The Shabak, I was told, is still against releasing the document. On February 15, 2005, I wrote to the Shabak spokesperson requesting that they reevaluate the classified nature of the report. Several days later she responded. The Shabak had no objection to the report being made public. And so it was.

AUTHOR'S NOTE

When I began this book, it proved difficult to penetrate the Mossad's wall of silence surrounding the assassination operation following the Munich Massacre. Gradually, I earned the trust of a few key officers; I also learned that I was the first person outside their inner circle that they had spoken to. Their trust earned me the confidence of others. I thus, in the course of researching this book, conducted extensive interviews with more than fifty individuals, including ex-heads of units in the Mossad and Israeli Intelligence; former combatants and senior analysts; and former heads of the Mossad. I also spoke with high-ranking officials on the Palestinian side. Most of my sources insisted on anonymity, for their own safety and protection. In some cases I have changed their names or referred to them by initials. For purposes of accuracy, I sometimes, when I felt it necessary, gave individuals described the opportunity to review my account and to comment on it. When possible, interviews were cross-checked for accuracy. I also examined internal and top secret government documents such as the Kopel Report and examined firsthand many of the sites described in this book, from Paris to Munich. In some cases, for dramatic effect, minor details of certain instances have been changed, in keeping with the known habits and demeanor of participants.

ACKNOWLEDGMENTS

Some of the sources that helped me write this book prefer not to be thanked in writing. For these former Mossad, Military Intelligence, and Shabak officers, secrecy is both habit and necessity. They would have liked their names in print, but fear of revenge, exacted on them and their family members by the children and grandchildren of the assassinated, kept them from revealing their name and rank, and I have obscured both in these pages. I could not in good conscience assuage that fear. All I can do is thank them anonymously for their willingness to reveal, assist, explain, and correct my descriptions of events they took part in. More remains unknown than known, but thanks to these officers, analysts, combatants, and commanders, the public is given the opportunity to examine previously unviewed episodes from within their covert world. These dedicated, uniformly shrewd people, many of whom I now consider as friends, did this without taking credit. In an effort to preserve their anonymity, I've changed some of their names.

This is also the place to thank all of my supportive friends and acquaintances, who provided invaluable help during the research and writing stages of the manuscript, enriching it with their insights, comments, and corrections: Colonel (res.) Amnon Biran, Colonel (res.) Muki Betzer, Yossi Smandar, Yoav and Orly Simon, Shlomi Kenan, Netta Ziv-Av, Aviv Levy, Nitza Tzameret, Ofer Lefler, Moshe Shai, Naomi Politzer, and Shimshon Issaki in Israel; Felice Maranz and Yaala Ariel-Joel in the United States; Guy Cohen in Munich; and François Gibault and Yael Scemama, my French connections in Paris.

Special thanks to Colonel (res.) Avner Druck, for his extended and genuine efforts; Colonel (res.) Yossi Daskal, for his balanced perspective; Ziv Koren, our talented and well-connected photography editor; Ankie Spitzer, for unconditionally opening her heart and sharing her experiences; Lisa Beyer, for her endless insight and encouragement; Matt Rees, Jerusalem's *Time* magazine bureau chief, for all his guidance and professional insights; Jean Max, for her sharp editing eye; Mitch Ginsburg, for his tireless wit, faithful translation, and dedication to the mission; Deborah Harris, my ceaselessly supportive agent, for granting me the opportunity to tackle this project; Philippa Brophy, our American agent, who oversees the important details of our lives; Will Murphy, my editor, a brilliant man, who conjured the idea of writing this book well before it became popular.

Final thanks to my family: my dear mother, Atara Klein, who listened night after night to my progress reports and offered unwavering support; to my beloved daughter, Nitzan, who peppered me with eye-opening questions and is the light of my life; and, ultimately, to my incomparable wife, Michal, who questioned, analyzed, advised, and unflinchingly accepted the role of husband and wife at home for the past few months.

AARON J. KLEIN is *Time* magazine's military and intelligence affairs correspondent in the Jerusalem Bureau. He was the recipient of the 2002 Henry Luce Award and has been a consultant for CNN.

Klein teaches a course in the relationship between media and the military establishment at the Hebrew University of Jerusalem's Master's Program. He was the military/security correspondent and analyst for *Hadashot* and *Al-Hamishmar,* two of Israel's leading national newspapers. He is a contributor to *Malam,* the journal for former IDF Intelligence, Mossad, and Internal Security Agency officers.

Aaron Klein holds an M.A. in history from the Hebrew University and is a captain in the IDF's Intelligence.

Klein, who lives in Jerusalem, is married and has a daughter.